OXFORD STUDE

Series Editor: Ste

John Keats
Selected Poems

Edited by Deborah West

Consultant: Victor Lee

Oxford University Press

OXFORD
UNIVERSITY PRESS

Great Clarendon Street, Oxford OX2 6DP

Oxford University Press is a department of the University of Oxford.
It furthers the University's objective of excellence in research, scholarship,
and education by publishing worldwide in

Oxford   New York

Auckland   Cape Town   Dar es Salaam   Hong Kong   Karachi
Kuala Lumpur   Madrid   Melbourne   Mexico City   Nairobi
New Delhi   Shanghai   Taipei   Toronto

With offices in

Argentina   Austria   Brazil   Chile   Czech Republic   France   Greece
Guatemala   Hungary   Italy   Japan   South Korea   Poland   Portugal
Singapore   Switzerland   Thailand   Turkey   Ukraine   Vietnam

Oxford is a registered trade mark of Oxford University Press
in the UK and in certain other countries

British Library Cataloguing in Publication Data
Data available

ISBN: 978-0-19-832546-8

10

Typeset by Palimpsest Book Production Ltd, Grangemouth, Stirlingshire
Printed in Great Britain by Clays Ltd., Bungay

The publishers would like to thank the following for permission to reproduce
photographs: P2 Mary Evans Picture Library; p3 Mary Evans Picture Library; p5t
Bridgeman Art Library; p5b Philippa Lewis/Edifice/Corbis UK Ltd; p144t Mary Evans
Picture Library; p144b Bridgeman Art Library; p199 Mary Evans Picture Library; p200 Mary
Evans Picture Library; p215 Mary Evans Picture Library; p216 Bill Ross/Corbis.

Contents

The Fall of Hyperion: A Dream   131

Acknowledgements

The poems are taken from *John Keats, The Complete Poems* edited by John Barnard (3rd edition, Penguin 2003). Extracts from *Letters of John Keats: A Selection* edited by Robert Gittings (Oxford Letters & Memoirs Series, OUP, New York, 1970), are reprinted by permission of Oxford University Press.

Deborah West would like to thank Leslie West for all his help and support in her endeavours.

Editors

Steven Croft, the series editor, holds degrees from Leeds and Sheffield universities. He has taught at secondary and tertiary level and is currently head of the Department of English and Humanities in a tertiary college. He has 25 years' examining experience at A level and is currently a Principal Examiner for English. He has written several books on teaching English at A level, and his publications for Oxford University Press include *Literature, Criticism and Style, Success in AQA Language and Literature* and *Exploring Language and Literature.*

Deborah West has degrees from both Sheffield University and The Shakespeare Institute, Stratford-upon-Avon, having reached doctoral standard. She has taught in further and higher education, and is currently Co-ordinator of English Literature in a tertiary college. She has worked as an A level examiner for several years, and is a Senior Examiner for English. Her publications include several A level texts for the National Extension College.

Foreword

Oxford Student Texts, under the founding editorship of Victor Lee, have established a reputation for presenting literary texts to students in both a scholarly and an accessible way. The new editions aim to build on this successful approach. They have been written to help students, particularly those studying English literature for AS or A level, to develop an increased understanding of their texts. Each volume in the series, which covers a selection of key poetry and drama texts, consists of four main sections which link together to provide an integrated approach to the study of the text.

The first part provides important background information about the writer, his or her times and the factors that played an important part in shaping the work. This discussion sets the work in context and explores some key contextual factors.

This section is followed by the poetry or play itself. The text is presented without accompanying notes so that students can engage with it on their own terms without the influence of secondary ideas. To encourage this approach, the Notes are placed in the third section, immediately following the text. The Notes provide explanations of particular words, phrases, images, allusions and so forth, to help students gain a full understanding of the text. They also raise questions or highlight particular issues or ideas which are important to consider when arriving at interpretations.

The fourth section, Interpretations, goes on to discuss a range of issues in more detail. This involves an examination of the influence of contextual factors as well as looking at such aspects as language and style, and various critical views or interpretations. A range of activities for students to carry out, together with discussions as to how these might be approached, are integrated into this section.

At the end of each volume there is a selection of Essay Questions, a Further Reading list and, where appropriate, a Glossary.

We hope you enjoy reading this text and working with these supporting materials, and wish you every success in your studies.

Steven Croft *Series Editor*

John Keats in Context

The life of John Keats

John Keats was born on 31 October 1795 in Finsbury, North London. His family was respectably middle class – his father, Thomas, was the chief hostler of a successful livery stable, the Swan and Hoop, and his mother, Frances Jennings, was the daughter of the proprietor of the stables. John was the oldest of four children, who were always devoted to one another.

In 1803, Keats enrolled at John Clarke's school in Enfield. With only about 75 boys in attendance, Keats received a very good education there, and the liberalist Clarke probably had a strong influence over the impressionable young boy. At school, Keats read widely and completed a translation of Virgil's *Aeneid*. Despite this, he was not known for his academic ability, but rather for his fighting prowess – even though he was barely five feet tall. His height was clearly a source of unhappiness for the young Keats, who later wrote, 'My mind has been the most discontented and restless one that ever was put into a body too small for it'.

After Keats's father died in 1804 in a horse-riding accident, his mother Frances married a bank clerk – but this second marriage did not last. Her second husband sold the stables, leaving her without a home. Ultimately, Frances was forced to move with her children – John, Fanny, George and Tom – to live with her mother in the village of Edmonton, just outside London. Frances flitted in and out of her children's lives over the next few years, until she died of tuberculosis in 1810.

After his mother's death, Keats's love of reading grew. It was probably further fostered under the tutelage and friendship of Cowden Clarke, who had taught Keats at school in Enfield and then introduced him to poetry and music. It was said to have been Clarke's copy of Edmund Spenser's epic poem *The Faerie Queene* that stimulated Keats to become deeply interested in verse. One

A portrait of John Keats by Joseph Severn, 1819

of his earliest poems, *Lines in Imitation of Spenser*, showed the deep impression the Renaissance poet made upon him.

In 1811, Keats decided to become a doctor, and became apprenticed to the apothecary-surgeon, Thomas Hammond. He ended this apprenticeship in 1815, and studied at Guy's Hospital for six months. By July 1816, he became a Licentiate of the Society of Apothecaries and was permitted to practise as a junior house surgeon.

The market square in Enfield; Keats was at school there from 1803

In London, Keats went on to meet the poet John Hamilton Reynolds, and the essayist, journalist and poet, Leigh Hunt. The latter was the editor of the leading liberal magazine of the time, *The Examiner*, and he became a mentor and patron for the younger writer, the two of them sharing the same ideologies and beliefs: according to Hunt, 'We became intimate on the spot, and I found the young poet's heart as warm as his imagination' (*Lord Byron and Some of his Contemporaries*, 1828). Hunt introduced Keats to some of the other leading poets of the day – including Percy Bysshe Shelley – and was so impressed by Keats's work that he published his sonnet O *Solitude* in the magazine.

By early 1817, Keats's love of poetry had increased so much that he gave up a career in medicine in order to pursue it. His first volume of poetry was published by Shelley's publishers, Charles and James Ollier, in that year, but it received poor reviews (despite containing *On First Looking into Chapman's Homer*). About this time, Keats began to use letters as the medium by which he communicated his thoughts and emotions. These letters, sent to friends and family, tell us a lot about the man and his poems.

Keats then turned his attention to the composition of a long poem, which he published in April 1818. Written in Elizabethan style, it is a 4,000-line narrative about the love between the moon goddess, Diana, and the young shepherd boy of the title, *Endymion*. Although it received very poor reviews – not least because Keats's liberal politics gave him a bad name in the Tory climate of the day – Keats was determined to continue. In a letter to Richard Woodhouse, he insisted, 'I am ambitious of doing the world some good: if I should be spared that may be the work of maturer years – in the interval I will assay to reach to as high a summit in Poetry as the nerve bestowed upon me will suffer.'

In the summer of 1818, a walking tour of the Lake District, Scotland and a short trip to Ireland helped to further forge Keats's respect for, and love of, the countryside, a topic he would engage with in his poetry. During this trip, it is said that Keats had to endure many a hardship with his friend Charles Brown; and sleeping outdoors in cold temperatures may well have weakened him.

In September 1818, Keats embarked upon a new long, narrative poem: *Hyperion*. At the same time, he was nursing his sick brother Tom, who died of tuberculosis in December of that year. His death is said to be one of the reasons why Keats abandoned the writing of *Hyperion*.

After Tom's death, Keats went to live with Charles Brown at Hampstead, where he met and fell in love with Fanny Brawne – to whom he was to become secretly engaged. In the winter of 1818–1819, Keats wrote *The Eve of St Agnes* and *The Eve of St Mark*, while in April–May 1819 he produced some of his most famous works, including the odes. In the same year, he completed *Lamia*, and went on to write another version of *Hyperion*, called *The Fall of Hyperion*.

In 1820, the second volume of Keats's poems was published. This time, it did receive critical acclaim. However, Keats was suffering from numerous problems. He had broken off his engagement to Fanny Brawne because he was too poor to marry her, and his general level of health had been gradually deteriorating. He felt obliged to follow the advice of two doctors,

Fanny Brawne, in an 1833 miniature

Keats shared part of Wentworth Place, Hampstead, with his friend
Charles Brown from the end of 1818

and so he set sail for Italy on 17 September, 1820, with his friend, the painter Joseph Severn. Keats declined Shelley's invitation to join him in Pisa and instead arrived in Rome on 15 November, where he settled into the Casina Rossa at number 26 Piazza di Spagna. Tragically, Keats died there on 23 February, 1821, at the age of 25.

He was buried in the Protestant Cemetery in Rome. Keats had instructed that on his tombstone be inscribed the ironic words: 'Here lies one whose name was writ in water'. There is no name or date; a Greek lyre with four of its eight strings broken is carved above the inscription.

John Keats and Fanny Brawne

There is much evidence that John Keats did not feel comfortable in the company of women, and that he was suspicious of their motives and their worthiness as human beings. In a letter dated July 1818, he wrote:

> When I am among Women I have evil thoughts, malice spleen – I cannot speak or be silent – I am full of Suspicions and therefore listen to no thing. I am in a hurry to be gone – You must be charitable and put all this perversity to my being disappointed since Boyhood... I could say a good deal about this but I will leave it in hopes of better and more worthy dispositions – and also content that I am wronging no one, for after all I do think better of Womankind than to suppose they care whether Mister John Keats five feet high likes them or not.

In another letter, dated October of the same year, Keats professed to hope that he would never marry, 'though the most beautiful Creature were waiting for me'. Rather, he imagined a more abstract idea 'of Beauty in all things', which seemed to satisfy him: 'No sooner am I alone than shapes of epic greatness are stationed around me, and serve my Spirit'.

While voicing such feelings, Keats had become secretly engaged to Fanny Brawne. They had first been introduced in September 1818, when he was almost 23 and she just 18, and it was to Fanny that he wrote a deluge of passionate letters as expressions of his joy at having met her. He spoke of his love in metaphorical terms, as being a force that he could not prevent, and an illness that only she could cure. Refuting her claims that it was only her physical beauty with which he was obsessed, Keats argued that she had 'a heart naturally furnish'd with wings [that sought to] imprison itself with me'. Although engaged, it seems that they never consummated their relationship. Keats was aware that he had to be in a financially stable position to marry, and with the knowledge that his tuberculosis (then called 'consumption') was probably to be fatal, he had ultimately to break off the engagement. Despite this, and the fact that he saw marriage as part of a world which may well stifle his artistic expression, Keats eagerly urged her to visit him, 'whenever you know me to be alone, come, no matter what day'.

Keats last saw Fanny Brawne in September 1820, a little before he left for Italy. On Keats's death, her love letters were buried with him, so that we will only ever understand their relationship from his point of view. Fanny did, however, write a letter to Keats's sister, expressing her regret that she had been separated from Keats when he died, and her belief that he was now at peace. She was adamant that no one knew how much he had really suffered during his short life.

Fanny Brawne went on to marry the novelist, Valentin Llanos, in 1826, having three children and living to the age of 65.

Romanticism

It is very important that we do not over-generalize when referring to 'Romanticism'. There is no consensus on a definition for the term 'Romantic', even though its use since the seventeenth and eighteenth centuries has carried a whole list of connotations, including *fable-like, fairy tale-like, dream-like, the absurd* and *the incredible*. The German writer and critic Friedrich Schiller (1759–1805) is said to have first used the term 'Romantic' to mean the opposite of 'Classical'; in other words, the opposite of the period that had come before Romanticism. Writers of that period, such as John Dryden, Alexander Pope, Joseph Addison, Jonathan Swift, Samuel Johnson, Oliver Goldsmith and Edmund Burke, had a strong sense of traditionalism and were often called 'Neoclassicists'. Writers were generally seen to abide by strict rules of poetry (and decorum), and sought to be measured in their approach to writing as in all things.

The German Romantic critic and scholar, August Wilhelm von Schlegel (1767–1845), soon sought to make the definition clearer, writing, 'the characteristic quality of "romanticism" is [a] union of opposite or discordant qualities.' Schlegel said that the Romantics preferred innovation to traditionalism, and mirroring what the individual feels rather than showing what all men do.

Some critics further limit the definition to cover only a very narrow period, 1770–1830, even confining Romanticism to the time of the outbreak of the French Revolution in 1789, or alternatively the publication of William Wordsworth and Samuel Taylor Coleridge's revolutionary volume *Lyrical Ballads* in 1798. The *Preface* to this work, written by Wordsworth in September 1800, was said to be a 'manifesto' of sorts, denouncing the poetic language of the century before. Wordsworth insisted that everyone and everything should be considered worthy subjects for art, and that poets should not be concerned about violating literary decorum, as the Neoclassicists had insisted. Rather, the only criterion for good poetry should be that it was 'the spontaneous overflow of powerful feelings' written in 'the real language of men'. Keats believed the same, once writing that 'if Poetry comes not as naturally as the Leaves to a tree it had better not come at all' (letter to John Taylor, 27 February, 1818).

Clearly, it is not very helpful to make one category out of all the writers of the late eighteenth and early nineteenth centuries. When Keats was born, William Blake was 37 years old, Wordsworth was 25 and Coleridge was 23. While it is true that they share many characteristics, both in terms of their ideologies and poetic techniques, it is evident that each man's ideologies and poetic techniques changed with time, and that not all of them agreed with the philosophies of the others. It is, therefore, very important to remember their differences:

> Keats was born over a livery stable, the Swan and Hoop, in north London, whereas Shelley was born on the family estate at Field Place, Warnham, in Sussex. Byron was a Cambridge graduate, whereas Blake never went to school. Coleridge was a life-long Christian, whereas Keats was an atheist. Byron was an aristocrat, whereas Keats was sometimes sneered at as a cockney. Blake was in lodgings in Soho at a time when Shelley was lodging at a palace in Pisa. The government that tried Blake for sedition was the same government as appointed Wordsworth Distributor of Stamps for Westmoreland. Coleridge was the son of a vicar and thought about becoming a minister himself in a church that Blake angrily dismissed as a conspiracy against the people.
>
> Paul O'Flinn, *How to Study Romantic Literature*

These differences show that all the so-called Romantic poets came from diverse backgrounds, which gave them diverse ideologies. Indeed, Aiden Day argues in his book *Romanticism* that 'any such attempts to summarise Romanticism inevitably end up over-systematising and simplifying the phenomenon. They imply a coherence... which closer inspection leads us to question.'

It has also been argued that to unify the Romantics under one definition is to ignore the fact that many of the so-called Romantic beliefs and defining features are not compatible. For example, the revolutions sweeping Europe were said to be a reaction against Neoclassical philosophies, but many of these philosophies actually inspired the revolutions, and were not dissimilar to the philosophies of the next 'era'.

It might be useful to see Romanticism as a psychological change rather than an ideological one. Some of the same yearnings, thoughts and optimistic feelings were certainly evident in the Neoclassical period, but the difference is marked in that the Romantics believed that changes for the better could actually be made:

> The cataclysmic nature of these changes means that literature, and in particular, poetry, ceased to be a decorative or peripheral thing, and became central in a quite new way as people looked for a focus for the new pictures of man.
>
> **Aiden Day,** *Romanticism*

By this definition, Romanticism perceives and responds to societal issues and problems in a new, more direct way.

To accept any single definition of Romanticism is, of course, to over-simplify a very complex issue. It is more important to examine the events and ideologies of the period and how they impacted upon the work of Keats and some of his contemporaries. Generalizations should always take second place to study of the poet and his or her own historical framework. Only then can a true picture of the poet and the possible interpretations of the poems be formed.

Society in John Keats's time

Keats was writing from 1818 until he died in 1821. We can therefore say that he was part of the second wave of Romanticism. The first wave evolved during his childhood. Although Romanticism existed all over Europe, the first wave of the movement in Britain included:

- William Wordsworth
- Samuel Taylor Coleridge
- William Blake.

The second wave included:
* George Gordon, Lord Byron
* Percy Bysshe Shelley
* John Keats.

Keats, like his fellow Romantics, embraced the power of the imagination, freedom of individual expression, sincerity and spontaneity. Convention and conservative morality, which the Romantics saw in eighteenth-century Neoclassicism and the ordered rationality of the Enlightenment, had resulted in detached and artificial emotions. Instead, Romanticism was in favour of asserting the self, with directness and intensity.

It is important that we place the Romantic poets against a backdrop of the politics, economy and social attitudes of the day. Many writers took a stand against authoritarian rule and repression, enslavement and poverty. Rooting their writing in reality, Keats and the other Romantic poets believed that change could come about in the here and now. Using nature to reinforce the power of the imagination – and therefore their poetry – gave each of them the voice to speak about human suffering, and the tools to ease it.

The writers of the time often involved themselves directly with politics. Here are some examples.
* The writer Thomas Paine (1737–1809) was exiled for producing *Rights of Man*, in 1791.
* In 1792, the essayist and poet Robert Southey (1774–1843) was expelled from Westminster School for writing against corporal punishment.
* Meanwhile, Mary Wollstonecraft (1759–1797) had written her *Vindication of the Rights of Woman* (1792), causing censure and outrage among conservative society. Using the ideologies behind the French Revolution, the text outlined the fact that women had no political rights – and that such oppression had to end.
* Keats's friend, the journalist Leigh Hunt (1784–1859), was

    imprisoned for two years from 1813 for the crime of libelling the Prince Regent.

- The government considered Coleridge (1772–1834) a maverick, not least because in 1795 he issued an anti-war lecture.
- Wordsworth (1770–1850) and his sister Dorothy (1771–1855) were believed to be radicals and, in 1798, were hounded out of their home in Alfoxden.
- Blake (1757–1827) was arrested and tried for sedition in 1804.
- Shelley (1792–1822) was almost murdered by a government spy.
- Byron (1788–1824) was exiled, and died while fighting for the cause of Greek independence.

From this by no means exhaustive list, it should be clear that the Romantics did not merely write frivolous or fanciful texts that sought to retreat from an unpleasant reality. On the whole, they attempted to highlight social ills, and move others to challenge them.

Analysing Keats's poetry

All examination boards will require of you the same rigours of written accuracy, fluency of argument and development of analysis; and, similarly, all will expect you to place your close reading of John Keats against his early nineteenth-century backdrop.

Contexts

Contexts are the conditions and circumstances that help to shape something, in this case a poem. Here are some examples:

- the circumstances of Keats's life, which may well have affected his writing, such as his gradually deteriorating health and the early deaths of many family members
- specific socio-political events that are referred to, either directly or indirectly, in his poems, such as the three main revolutions of the day, which adversely affected the already under-privileged
- the literary context of Keats's work, and whether it can be said that his method of writing is 'Romantic'
- the context of one poem with reference to Keats's poetry as a whole body of work: for example, examining one of his odes in light of it being a progression in style from one of his sonnets
- the context of one poem in relation to one or more others, such as comparing two or more of Keats's poems about death
- the style and structure of Keats's poetry, and whether he was in any way groundbreaking when compared to other poets of the time: for example, the way in which he made the ode genre his own.

Analysis

You will need to be able to explore, examine in detail and write a developed argument on Keats's techniques and the devices used to express his ideas. This is a three-step process:
  1 identify a literary or linguistic device
  2 evidence it
  3 explain the significance of its use to the poem as a whole.

There can be more than one interpretation of any idea; as long as you can provide a logical explanation, and provide evidence for your argument, you will be awarded marks.

Comparison

For some examination boards you will be expected to make a comparison between two or more texts. This will involve seeking out the similarities and differences, and commenting upon the effects of these relationships. Examiners prefer an academic response to sustain the comparison throughout, in order that candidates do not fall into the trap of analysing poems separately.

Independent opinions and judgements

You are asked to deliver your own opinions and judgements on the poems you are studying, and in order to do so successfully you must provide relevant examples. You must demonstrate that you are aware that there are different interpretations, and that your view is just one of many possibilities.

Selected Poems of John Keats

On First Looking into Chapman's Homer

Much have I travelled in the realms of gold,
    And many goodly states and kingdoms seen;
    Round many western islands have I been
Which bards in fealty to Apollo hold.
5 Oft of one wide expanse had I been told
    That deep-browed Homer ruled as his demesne;
    Yet did I never breathe its pure serene
Till I heard Chapman speak out loud and bold:
Then felt I like some watcher of the skies
10   When a new planet swims into his ken;
Or like stout Cortez when with eagle eyes
    He stared at the Pacific – and all his men
Looked at each other with a wild surmise –
    Silent, upon a peak in Darien.

Keen, Fitful Gusts

Keen, fitful gusts are whispering here and there
    Among the bushes half leafless, and dry;
    The stars look very cold about the sky,
And I have many miles on foot to fare.
5 Yet feel I little of the cool bleak air,
    Or of the dead leaves rustling drearily,
    Or of those silver lamps that burn on high,
Or of the distance from home's pleasant lair:
For I am brimful of the friendliness

10   That in a little cottage I have found;
     Of fair-haired Milton's eloquent distress,
       And all his love for gentle Lycid drowned;
     Of lovely Laura in her light green dress,
       And faithful Petrarch gloriously crowned.

To my Brothers

Small, busy flames play through the fresh-laid coals,
   And their faint cracklings o'er our silence creep
   Like whispers of the household gods that keep
A gentle empire o'er fraternal souls.
5 And while, for rhymes, I search around the poles,
   Your eyes are fixed, as in poetic sleep,
   Upon the lore so voluble and deep,
That aye at fall of night our care condoles.
This is your birth-day Tom, and I rejoice
10   That thus it passes smoothly, quietly.
Many such eves of gently whispering noise
   May we together pass, and calmly try
What are this world's true joys – ere the great voice,
   From its fair face, shall bid our spirits fly.

To Haydon

Great spirits now on earth are sojourning;
   He of the cloud, the cataract, the lake,
   Who on Helvellyn's summit, wide awake,
Catches his freshness from Archangel's wing:
5 He of the rose, the violet, the spring,
   The social smile, the chain for Freedom's sake:
   And lo! – whose steadfastness would never take

A meaner sound than Raphael's whispering.
And other spirits there are standing apart
10   Upon the forehead of the age to come;
These, these will give the world another heart,
    And other pulses. Hear ye not the hum
Of mighty workings? –
    Listen awhile ye nations, and be dumb.

On the Grasshopper and Cricket

The poetry of earth is never dead:
    When all the birds are faint with the hot sun,
    And hide in cooling trees, a voice will run
From hedge to hedge about the new-mown mead –
5 That is the Grasshopper's. He takes the lead
    In summer luxury; he has never done
    With his delights, for when tired out with fun
He rests at ease beneath some pleasant weed.
The poetry of earth is ceasing never:
10   On a lone winter evening, when the frost
      Has wrought a silence, from the stove there shrills
The Cricket's song, in warmth increasing ever,
    And seems to one in drowsiness half lost,
      The Grasshopper's among some grassy hills.

On the Sea

It keeps eternal whisperings around
    Desolate shores, and with its mighty swell
    Gluts twice ten thousand caverns, till the spell
Of Hecate leaves them their old shadowy sound.
5 Often 'tis in such gentle temper found,

That scarcely will the very smallest shell
Be moved for days from where it sometime fell,
When last the winds of Heaven were unbound.
Oh ye! who have your eye-balls vexed and tired,
10   Feast them upon the wideness of the Sea –
        Oh ye! whose ears are dinned with uproar rude,
        Or fed too much with cloying melody –
        Sit ye near some old cavern's mouth and brood,
Until ye start, as if the sea-nymphs quired!

Endymion

A thing of beauty is a joy for ever:
Its loveliness increases; it will never
Pass into nothingness; but still will keep
A bower quiet for us, and a sleep
5   Full of sweet dreams, and health, and quiet breathing.
Therefore, on every morrow, are we wreathing
A flowery band to bind us to the earth,
Spite of despondence, of the inhuman dearth
Of noble natures, of the gloomy days,
10   Of all the unhealthy and o'er-darkened ways
Made for our searching: yes, in spite of all,
Some shape of beauty moves away the pall
From our dark spirits. Such the sun, the moon,
Trees old, and young, sprouting a shady boon
15   For simple sheep; and such are daffodils
With the green world they live in; and clear rills
That for themselves a cooling covert make
'Gainst the hot season; the mid forest brake,
Rich with a sprinkling of fair musk-rose blooms:
20   And such too is the grandeur of the dooms
We have imagined for the mighty dead;

All lovely tales that we have heard or read –
An endless fountain of immortal drink,
Pouring unto us from the heaven's brink.

* * *

O thou, whose mighty palace roof doth hang
From jagged trunks, and overshadoweth
Eternal whispers, glooms, the birth, life, death
235   Of unseen flowers in heavy peacefulness;
Who lov'st to see the hamadryads dress
Their ruffled locks where meeting hazels darken;
And through whole solemn hours dost sit, and hearken
The dreary melody of bedded reeds
240   In desolate places, where dank moisture breeds
The pipy hemlock to strange overgrowth;
Bethinking thee, how melancholy loth
Thou wast to lose fair Syrinx – do thou now –
By thy love's milky brow! –
245   By all the trembling mazes that she ran –
Hear us, great Pan!

O thou, for whose soul-soothing quiet, turtles
Passion their voices cooingly 'mong myrtles,
What time thou wanderest at eventide
250   Through sunny meadows, that outskirt the side
Of thine enmossèd realms: O thou, to whom
Broad-leavèd fig trees even now foredoom
Their ripened fruitage; yellow-girted bees
Their golden honeycombs; our village leas
255   Their fairest-blossomed beans and poppied corn;
The chuckling linnet its five young unborn
To sing for thee; low creeping strawberries
Their summer coolness; pent up butterflies
Their freckled wings; yea, the fresh budding year

260   All its completions – be quickly near,
     By every wind that nods the mountain pine,
     O forester divine!

     Thou, to whom every faun and satyr flies
     For willing service; whether to surprise
265   The squatted hare while in half-sleeping fit;
     Or upward ragged precipices flit
     To save poor lambkins from the eagle's maw;
     Or by mysterious enticement draw
     Bewildered shepherds to their path again;
270   Or to tread breathless round the frothy main,
     And gather up all fancifullest shells
     For thee to tumble into Naiads' cells,
     And, being hidden, laugh at their out-peeping;
     Or to delight thee with fantastic leaping,
275   The while they pelt each other on the crown
     With silvery oak apples, and fir cones brown –
     By all the echoes that about thee ring,
     Hear us, O satyr king!

     O Hearkener to the loud clapping shears,
280   While ever and anon to his shorn peers
     A ram goes bleating; Winder of the horn,
     When snouted wild-boars routing tender corn
     Anger our huntsmen; Breather round our farms,
     To keep off mildews, and all weather harms;
285   Strange ministrant of undescribèd sounds,
     That come a-swooning over hollow grounds,
     And wither drearily on barren moors;
     Dread opener of the mysterious doors
     Leading to universal knowledge – see,
290   Great son of Dryope,
     The many that are come to pay their vows
     With leaves about their brows!

Be still the unimaginable lodge
For solitary thinkings; such as dodge
295 Conception to the very bourne of heaven,
Then leave the naked brain; be still the leaven,
That spreading in this dull and clodded earth
Gives it a touch ethereal – a new birth;
Be still a symbol of immensity;
300 A firmament reflected in a sea;
An element filling the space between,
An unknown – but no more! we humbly screen
With uplift hands our foreheads, lowly bending,
And giving out a shout most heaven rending,
305 Conjure thee to receive our humble paean,
Upon thy Mount Lycean!

* * *

Wherein lies happiness? In that which becks
Our ready minds to fellowship divine,
A fellowship with essence; till we shine,
780 Full alchemized, and free of space. Behold
The clear religion of heaven! Fold
A rose leaf round thy finger's taperness,
And soothe thy lips: hist, when the airy stress
Of music's kiss impregnates the free winds,
785 And with a sympathetic touch unbinds
Aeolian magic from their lucid wombs;
Then old songs waken from enclouded tombs;
Old ditties sigh above their father's grave;
Ghosts of melodious prophesyings rave
790 Round every spot where trod Apollo's foot;
Bronze clarions awake, and faintly bruit,
Where long ago a giant battle was;
And, from the turf, a lullaby doth pass
In every place where infant Orpheus slept.

795 Feel we these things? – that moment have we stepped
Into a sort of oneness, and our state
Is like a floating spirit's. But there are
Richer entanglements, enthralments far
More self-destroying, leading, by degrees,
800 To the chief intensity: the crown of these
Is made of love and friendship, and sits high
Upon the forehead of humanity.
All its more ponderous and bulky worth
Is friendship, whence there ever issues forth
805 A steady splendour; but at the tip-top,
There hangs by unseen film, an orbèd drop
Of light, and that is love: its influence,
Thrown in our eyes, genders a novel sense,
At which we start and fret; till in the end,
810 Melting into its radiance, we blend,
Mingle, and so become a part of it –
Nor with aught else can our souls interknit
So wingedly. When we combine therewith,
Life's self is nourished by its proper pith,
815 And we are nurtured like a pelican brood.
Ay, so delicious is the unsating food,
That men, who might have towered in the van
Of all the congregated world, to fan
And winnow from the coming step of time
820 All chaff of custom, wipe away all slime
Left by men-slugs and human serpentry,
Have been content to let occasion die,
Whilst they did sleep in love's elysium.
And, truly, I would rather be struck dumb,
825 Than speak against this ardent listlessness:
For I have ever thought that it might bless
The world with benefits unknowingly,
As does the nightingale, up-perchèd high,

And cloistered among cool and bunchèd leaves –
830 She sings but to her love, nor e'er conceives
How tip-toe Night holds back her dark-grey hood.
Just so may love, although 'tis understood
The mere commingling of passionate breath,
Produce more than our searching witnesseth –
835 What I know not: but who, of men, can tell
That flowers would bloom, or that green fruit
      would swell
To melting pulp, that fish would have bright mail,
The earth its dower of river, wood, and vale,
The meadows runnels, runnels pebble-stones,
840 The seed its harvest, or the lute its tones,
Tones ravishment, or ravishment its sweet,
If human souls did never kiss and greet?

On Sitting Down to Read *King Lear* Once Again

O golden-tongued Romance, with serene lute!
    Fair plumèd Syren, Queen of far-away!
    Leave melodizing on this wintry day,
Shut up thine olden pages, and be mute:
5 Adieu! for, once again, the fierce dispute
    Betwixt damnation and impassioned clay
    Must I burn through, once more humbly assay
The bitter-sweet of this Shakespearian fruit:
Chief Poet! and ye clouds of Albion,
10   Begetters of our deep eternal theme!
When through the old oak forest I am gone,
    Let me not wander in a barren dream,
But, when I am consumèd in the fire,
Give me new Phoenix wings to fly at my desire.

23

When I have Fears

When I have fears that I may cease to be
  Before my pen has gleaned my teaming brain,
Before high-pilèd books, in charactery,
  Hold like rich garners the full-ripened grain;
5 When I behold, upon the night's starred face,
  Huge cloudy symbols of a high romance,
And think that I may never live to trace
  Their shadows, with the magic hand of chance;
And when I feel, fair creature of an hour!
10 That I shall never look upon thee more,
Never have relish in the faery power
  Of unreflecting love! – then on the shore
Of the wide world I stand alone, and think
Till love and fame to nothingness do sink.

Lines on the Mermaid Tavern

Souls of Poets dead and gone,
What Elysium have ye known,
Happy field or mossy cavern,
Choicer than the Mermaid Tavern?
5 Have ye tippled drink more fine
Than mine host's Canary wine?
Or are fruits of Paradise
Sweeter than those dainty pies
Of venison? O generous food!
10 Dressed as though bold Robin Hood
Would, with his maid Marian,
Sup and bowse from horn and can.

I have heard that on a day
Mine host's sign-board flew away,
15 Nobody knew whither, till
An astrologer's old quill
To a sheepskin gave the story,
Said he saw you in your glory,
Underneath a new-old sign
20 Sipping beverage divine,
And pledging with contented smack
The Mermaid in the Zodiac.

Souls of Poets dead and gone,
What Elysium have ye known,
25 Happy field or mossy cavern,
Choicer than the Mermaid Tavern?

Isabella, or The Pot of Basil
A story from Boccaccio

I
Fair Isabel, poor simple Isabel!
    Lorenzo, a young palmer in Love's eye!
They could not in the self-same mansion dwell
    Without some stir of heart, some malady;
5 They could not sit at meals but feel how well
    It soothed each to be the other by;
They could not, sure, beneath the same roof sleep
But to each other dream, and nightly weep.

II
With every morn their love grew tenderer,
10   With every eve deeper and tenderer still;
He might not in house, field, or garden stir,
    But her full shape would all his seeing fill;

25

And his continual voice was pleasanter
  To her than noise of trees or hidden rill;
15 Her lute-string gave an echo of his name,
She spoilt her half-done broidery with the same.

III
He knew whose gentle hand was at the latch
  Before the door had given her to his eyes;
And from her chamber-window he would catch
20 Her beauty farther than the falcon spies;
And constant as her vespers would he watch,
  Because her face was turned to the same skies;
And with sick longing all the night outwear,
To hear her morning-step upon the stair.

IV
25 A whole long month of May in this sad plight
  Made their cheeks paler by the break of June:
'To-morrow will I bow to my delight,
  To-morrow will I ask my lady's boon.'
'O may I never see another night,
30 Lorenzo, if thy lips breathe not love's tune.'
So spake they to their pillows; but, alas,
Honeyless days and days did he let pass –

V
Until sweet Isabella's untouched cheek
  Fell sick within the rose's just domain,
35 Fell thin as a young mother's, who doth seek
  By every lull to cool her infant's pain:
'How ill she is,' said he, 'I may not speak,
  And yet I will, and tell my love all plain:
If looks speak love-laws, I will drink her tears,
40 And at the least 'twill startle off her cares.'

VI
So said he one fair morning, and all day
　　His heart beat awfully against his side;
And to his heart he inwardly did pray
　　For power to speak; but still the ruddy tide
45　Stifled his voice, and pulsed resolve away –
　　Fevered his high conceit of such a bride,
Yet brought him to the meekness of a child:
Alas! when passion is both meek and wild!

VII
So once more he had waked and anguishèd
50　　A dreary night of love and misery,
If Isabel's quick eye had not been wed
　　To every symbol on his forehead high.
She saw it waxing very pale and dead,
　　And straight all flushed; so, lispèd tenderly,
55　'Lorenzo!' – here she ceased her timid quest,
But in her tone and look he read the rest.

VIII
'O Isabella, I can half-perceive
　　That I may speak my grief into thine ear.
If thou didst ever anything believe,
60　　Believe how I love thee, believe how near
My soul is to its doom: I would not grieve
　　Thy hand by unwelcome pressing, would not fear
Thine eyes by gazing; but I cannot live
Another night, and not my passion shrive.

IX
65　'Love! thou art leading me from wintry cold,
　　Lady! thou leadest me to summer clime,
And I must taste the blossoms that unfold

27

In its ripe warmth this gracious morning time.'
So said, his erewhile timid lips grew bold,
70   And poesied with hers in dewy rhyme:
Great bliss was with them, and great happiness
Grew, like a lusty flower, in June's caress.

X
Parting they seemed to tread upon the air,
    Twin roses by the zephyr blown apart
75   Only to meet again more close, and share
    The inward fragrance of each other's heart.
She, to her chamber gone, a ditty fair
    Sang, of delicious love and honeyed dart;
He with light steps went up a western hill,
80   And bade the sun farewell, and joyed his fill.

XI
All close they met again, before the dusk
    Had taken from the stars its pleasant veil,
All close they met, all eves, before the dusk
    Had taken from the stars its pleasant veil,
85   Close in a bower of hyacinth and musk,
    Unknown of any, free from whispering tale.
Ah! better had it been for ever so,
Than idle ears should pleasure in their woe.

XII
Were they unhappy then? – It cannot be –
90   Too many tears for lovers have been shed,
Too many sighs give we to them in fee,
    Too much of pity after they are dead,
Too many doleful stories do we see,
    Whose matter in bright gold were best be read;
95   Except in such a page where Theseus' spouse
Over the pathless waves towards him bows.

XIII
But, for the general award of love,
    The little sweet doth kill much bitterness;
Though Dido silent is in under-grove,
100   And Isabella's was a great distress,
Though young Lorenzo in warm Indian clove
    Was not embalmed, this truth is not the less –
Even bees, the little almsmen of spring-bowers,
Know there is richest juice in poison-flowers.

XIV
105 With her two brothers this fair lady dwelt,
    Enrichèd from ancestral merchandise,
And for them many a weary hand did swelt
    In torchèd mines and noisy factories,
And many once proud-quivered loins did melt
110   In blood from stinging whip – with hollow eyes
Many all day in dazzling river stood,
To take the rich-ored driftings of the flood.

XV
For them the Ceylon diver held his breath,
    And went all naked to the hungry shark;
115 For them his ears gushed blood; for them in death
    The seal on the cold ice with piteous bark
Lay full of darts; for them alone did seethe
    A thousand men in troubles wide and dark:
Half-ignorant, they turned an easy wheel,
120 That set sharp racks at work to pinch and peel.

XVI
Why were they proud? Because their marble founts
    Gushed with more pride than do a wretch's tears? –
Why were they proud? Because fair orange-mounts

Were of more soft ascent than lazar stairs? –
125 Why were they proud? Because red-lined accounts
Were richer than the songs of Grecian years? –
Why were they proud? again we ask aloud,
Why in the name of Glory were they proud?

XVII

Yet were these Florentines as self-retired
130   In hungry pride and gainful cowardice,
As two close Hebrews in that land inspired,
Paled in and vineyarded from beggar-spies –
The hawks of ship-mast forests – the untired
And panniered mules for ducats and old lies –
135 Quick cat's-paws on the generous stray-away –
Great wits in Spanish, Tuscan, and Malay.

XVIII

How was it these same ledger-men could spy
Fair Isabella in her downy nest?
How could they find out in Lorenzo's eye
140   A straying from his toil? Hot Egypt's pest
Into their vision covetous and sly!
How could these money-bags see east and west? –
Yet so they did – and every dealer fair
Must see behind, as doth the hunted hare.

XIX

145 O eloquent and famed Boccaccio!
Of thee we now should ask forgiving boon,
And of thy spicy myrtles as they blow,
And of thy roses amorous of the moon,
And of thy lilies, that do paler grow
150   Now they can no more hear thy gittern's tune.
For venturing syllables that ill beseem
The quiet glooms of such a piteous theme.

XX

Grant thou a pardon here, and then the tale
    Shall move on soberly, as it is meet;
155 There is no other crime, no mad assail
    To make old prose in modern rhyme more sweet:
But it is done – succeed the verse or fail –
    To honour thee, and thy gone spirit greet,
To stead thee as a verse in English tongue,
160 An echo of thee in the north wind sung.

XXI

These brethren having found by many signs
    What love Lorenzo for their sister had,
And how she loved him too, each unconfines
    His bitter thoughts to other, well nigh mad
165 That he, the servant of their trade designs,
    Should in their sister's love be blithe and glad,
When 'twas their plan to coax her by degrees
To some high noble and his olive-trees.

XXII

And many a jealous conference had they,
170   And many times they bit their lips alone,
Before they fixed upon a surest way
    To make the youngster for his crime atone;
And at the last, these men of cruel clay
    Cut Mercy with a sharp knife to the bone,
175 For they resolvèd in some forest dim
To kill Lorenzo, and there bury him.

XXIII

So on a pleasant morning, as he leant
    Into the sunrise, o'er the balustrade
Of the garden-terrace, towards him they bent

180   Their footing through the dews; and to him said,
       'You seem there in the quiet of content,
           Lorenzo, and we are most loth to invade
       Calm speculation; but if you are wise,
       Bestride your steed while cold is in the skies.

       XXIV
185   'To-day we purpose, ay, this hour we mount
           To spur three leagues towards the Apennine;
       Come down, we pray thee, ere the hot sun count
           His dewy rosary on the eglantine.'
       Lorenzo, courteously as he was wont,
190   Bowed a fair greeting to these serpents' whine;
       And went in haste, to get in readiness,
       With belt, and spur, and bracing huntsman's dress.

       XXV
       And as he to the court-yard passed along,
           Each third step did he pause, and listened oft
195   If he could hear his lady's matin-song,
           Or the light whisper of her footstep soft;
       And as he thus over his passion hung,
           He heard a laugh full musical aloft,
       When, looking up, he saw her features bright
200   Smile through an in-door lattice, all delight.

       XXVI
       'Love, Isabel!' said he, 'I was in pain
           Lest I should miss to bid thee a good morrow:
       Ah! what if I should lose thee, when so fain
           I am to stifle all the heavy sorrow
205   Of a poor three hours' absence? but we'll gain
           Out of the amorous dark what day doth borrow.
       Good bye! I'll soon be back.' 'Good bye!' said she –
       And as he went she chanted merrily.

XXVII
So the two brothers and their murdered man
210   Rode past fair Florence, to where Arno's stream
Gurgles through straitened banks, and still doth fan
    Itself with dancing bulrush, and the bream
Keeps head against the freshets. Sick and wan
    The brothers' faces in the ford did seem,
215 Lorenzo's flush with love. – They passed the water
Into a forest quiet for the slaughter.

XXVIII
There was Lorenzo slain and buried in,
    There in that forest did his great love cease.
Ah! when a soul doth thus its freedom win,
220   It aches in loneliness – is ill at peace
As the break-covert blood-hounds of such sin.
    They dipped their swords in the water, and did tease
Their horses homeward, with convulsèd spur,
Each richer by his being a murderer.

XXIX
225 They told their sister how, with sudden speed,
    Lorenzo had ta'en ship for foreign lands,
Because of some great urgency and need
    In their affairs, requiring trusty hands.
Poor girl! put on thy stifling widow's weed,
230   And 'scape at once from Hope's accursèd bands;
To-day thou wilt not see him, nor to-morrow,
And the next day will be a day of sorrow.

XXX
She weeps alone for pleasures not to be;
    Sorely she wept until the night came on,
235 And then, instead of love, O misery!

She brooded o'er the luxury alone:
His image in the dusk she seemed to see,
   And to the silence made a gentle moan,
   Spreading her perfect arms upon the air,
240 And on her couch low murmuring, 'Where? O where?'

XXXI

But Selfishness, Love's cousin, held not long
   Its fiery vigil in her single breast.
She fretted for the golden hour, and hung
   Upon the time with feverish unrest –
245 Not long – for soon into her heart a throng
   Of higher occupants, a richer zest,
Came tragic – passion not to be subdued,
And sorrow for her love in travels rude.

XXXII

In the mid days of autumn, on their eves
250   The breath of Winter comes from far away,
And the sick west continually bereaves
   Of some gold tinge, and plays a roundelay
Of death among the bushes and the leaves,
   To make all bare before he dares to stray
255 From his north cavern. So sweet Isabel
By gradual decay from beauty fell,

XXXIII

Because Lorenzo came not. Oftentimes
   She asked her brothers, with an eye all pale,
Striving to be itself, what dungeon climes
260   Could keep him off so long? They spake a tale
Time after time, to quiet her. Their crimes
   Came on them, like a smoke from Hinnom's vale;
And every night in dreams they groaned aloud,
To see their sister in her snowy shroud.

XXXIV

265 And she had died in drowsy ignorance,
     But for a thing more deadly dark than all.
  It came like a fierce potion, drunk by chance,
     Which saves a sick man from the feathered pall
  For some few gasping moments; like a lance,
270   Waking an Indian from his cloudy hall
  With cruel pierce, and bringing him again
  Sense of the gnawing fire at heart and brain.

XXXV

  It was a vision. – In the drowsy gloom,
     The dull of midnight, at her couch's foot
275 Lorenzo stood, and wept: the forest tomb
     Had marred his glossy hair which once could shoot
  Lustre into the sun, and put cold doom
     Upon his lips, and taken the soft lute
  From his lorn voice, and past his loamèd ears
280 Had made a miry channel for his tears.

XXXVI

  Strange sound it was, when the pale shadow spake;
     For there was striving, in its piteous tongue,
  To speak as when on earth it was awake,
     And Isabella on its music hung.
285 Languor there was in it, and tremulous shake,
     As in a palsied Druid's harp unstrung;
  And through it moaned a ghostly under-song,
  Like hoarse night-gusts sepulchral briars among.

XXXVII

  Its eyes, though wild, were still all dewy bright
290   With love, and kept all phantom fear aloof
  From the poor girl by magic of their light,

The while it did unthread the horrid woof
Of the late darkened time – the murderous spite
Of pride and avarice, the dark pine roof
295 In the forest, and the sodden turfèd dell,
Where, without any word, from stabs he fell.

XXXVIII
Saying moreover, 'Isabel, my sweet!
Red whortle-berries droop above my head,
And a large flint-stone weighs upon my feet;
300 Around me beeches and high chestnuts shed
Their leaves and prickly nuts; a sheep-fold bleat
Comes from beyond the river to my bed:
Go, shed one tear upon my heather-bloom,
And it shall comfort me within the tomb.

XXXIX
305 'I am a shadow now, alas! alas!
Upon the skirts of human-nature dwelling
Alone. I chant alone the holy mass,
While little sounds of life are round me knelling,
And glossy bees at noon do fieldward pass,
310 And many a chapel bell the hour is telling,
Paining me through: those sounds grow strange to me,
And thou art distant in humanity.

XL
'I know what was, I feel full well what is,
And I should rage if spirits could go mad;
315 Though I forget the taste of earthly bliss,
That paleness warms my grave, as though I had
A seraph chosen from the bright abyss
To be my spouse: thy paleness makes me glad;
Thy beauty grows upon me, and I feel
320 A greater love through all my essence steal.'

XLI

The Spirit mourn'd 'Adieu!' – dissolved and left
　　The atom darkness in a slow turmoil;
As when of healthful midnight sleep bereft,
　　Thinking on rugged hours and fruitless toil,
325 We put our eyes into a pillowy cleft,
　　And see the spangly gloom froth up and boil:
It made sad Isabella's eyelids ache,
And in the dawn she started up awake –

XLII

'Ha! ha!' said she, 'I knew not this hard life,
330 　I thought the worst was simple misery;
I thought some Fate with pleasure or with strife
　　Portioned us – happy days, or else to die;
But there is crime – a brother's bloody knife!
　　Sweet Spirit, thou hast schooled my infancy:
335 I'll visit thee for this, and kiss thine eyes,
And greet thee morn and even in the skies.'

XLIII

When the full morning came, she had devised
　　How she might secret to the forest hie;
How she might find the clay, so dearly prized,
340 　And sing to it one latest lullaby;
How her short absence might be unsurmised,
　　While she the inmost of the dream would try.
Resolved, she took with her an agèd nurse,
And went into that dismal forest-hearse.

XLIV

345 See, as they creep along the river side,
　　How she doth whisper to that agèd dame,
And, after looking round the champaign wide,

37

Shows her a knife. – 'What feverous hectic flame
Burns in thee, child? – What good can thee betide,
350   That thou shouldst smile again?' The evening came,
And they had found Lorenzo's earthy bed –
The flint was there, the berries at his head.

XLV
Who hath not loitered in a green church-yard,
    And let his spirit, like a demon-mole,
355 Work through the clayey soil and gravel hard,
    To see skull, coffined bones, and funeral stole;
Pitying each form that hungry Death hath marred
    And filling it once more with human soul?
Ah! this is holiday to what was felt
360 When Isabella by Lorenzo knelt.

XLVI
She gazed into the fresh-thrown mould, as though
    One glance did fully all its secrets tell;
Clearly she saw, as other eyes would know
    Pale limbs at bottom of a crystal well;
365 Upon the murderous spot she seemed to grow,
    Like to a native lily of the dell –
Then with her knife, all sudden, she began
To dig more fervently than misers can.

XLVII
Soon she turned up a soilèd glove, whereon
370   Her silk had played in purple phantasies,
She kissed it with a lip more chill than stone,
    And put it in her bosom, where it dries
And freezes utterly unto the bone
    Those dainties made to still an infant's cries:
375 Then 'gan she work again, nor stayed her care,
But to throw back at times her veiling hair.

XLVIII

That old nurse stood beside her wondering,
    Until her heart felt pity to the core
At sight of such a dismal labouring,
380   And so she kneelèd, with her locks all hoar,
And put her lean hands to the horrid thing.
    Three hours they laboured at this travail sore –
At last they felt the kernel of the grave,
And Isabella did not stamp and rave.

XLIX

385 Ah! wherefore all this wormy circumstance?
    Why linger at the yawning tomb so long?
O for the gentleness of old Romance,
    The simple plaining of a minstrel's song!
Fair reader, at the old tale take a glance,
390   For here, in truth, it doth not well belong
To speak – O turn thee to the very tale,
And taste the music of that vision pale.

L

With duller steel than the Persèan sword
    They cut away no formless monster's head,
395 But one, whose gentleness did well accord
    With death, as life. The ancient harps have said,
Love never dies, but lives, immortal Lord:
    If Love impersonate was ever dead,
Pale Isabella kissed it, and low moaned.
400 'Twas Love – cold, dead indeed, but not dethroned.

LI

In anxious secrecy they took it home,
    And then the prize was all for Isabel.
She calmed its wild hair with a golden comb,

And all around each eye's sepulchral cell
405 Pointed each fringèd lash; the smeared loam
With tears, as chilly as a dripping well,
She drenched away – and still she combed, and kept
Sighing all day – and still she kissed, and wept.

LII

Then in a silken scarf – sweet with the dews
410 Of precious flowers plucked in Araby,
And divine liquids come with odorous ooze
Through the cold serpent-pipe refreshfully –
She wrapped it up; and for its tomb did choose
A garden-pot, wherein she laid it by,
415 And covered it with mould, and o'er it set
Sweet basil, which her tears kept ever wet.

LIII

And she forgot the stars, the moon, and sun,
And she forgot the blue above the trees,
And she forgot the dells where waters run,
420 And she forgot the chilly autumn breeze;
She had no knowledge when the day was done,
And the new morn she saw not, but in peace
Hung over her sweet basil evermore,
And moistened it with tears unto the core.

LIV

425 And so she ever fed it with thin tears,
Whence thick, and green, and beautiful it grew,
So that it smelt more balmy than its peers
Of basil-tufts in Florence; for it drew
Nurture besides, and life, from human fears,
430 From the fast mouldering head there shut from view:
So that the jewel, safely casketed,
Came forth, and in perfumèd leafits spread.

LV

O Melancholy, linger here awhile!
  O Music, Music, breathe despondingly!
435 O Echo, Echo, from some sombre isle,
  Unknown, Lethean, sigh to us – O sigh!
Spirits in grief, lift up your heads, and smile.
  Lift up your heads, sweet Spirits, heavily,
And make a pale light in your cypress glooms,
440 Tinting with silver wan your marble tombs.

LVI

Moan hither, all ye syllables of woe,
  From the deep throat of sad Melpomene!
Through bronzèd lyre in tragic order go,
  And touch the strings into a mystery;
445 Sound mournfully upon the winds and low;
  For simple Isabel is soon to be
Among the dead. She withers, like a palm
Cut by an Indian for its juicy balm.

LVII

O leave the palm to wither by itself;
450   Let not quick Winter chill its dying hour! –
It may not be – those Baälites of pelf,
  Her brethren, noted the continual shower
From her dead eyes; and many a curious elf,
  Among her kindred, wondered that such dower
455 Of youth and beauty should be thrown aside
By one marked out to be a Noble's bride.

LVIII

And, furthermore, her brethren wondered much
  Why she sat drooping by the basil green,
And why it flourished, as by magic touch.

460 Greatly they wondered what the thing might mean:
They could not surely give belief, that such
   A very nothing would have power to wean
Her from her own fair youth, and pleasures gay,
And even remembrance of her love's delay.

LIX

465 Therefore they watched a time when they might sift
   This hidden whim; and long they watched in vain:
For seldom did she go to chapel-shrift,
   And seldom felt she any hunger-pain;
And when she left, she hurried back, as swift
470   As bird on wing to breast its eggs again;
And, patient as a hen-bird, sat her there
Beside her basil, weeping through her hair.

LX

Yet they contrived to steal the basil-pot,
   And to examine it in secret place.
475 The thing was vile with green and livid spot,
   And yet they knew it was Lorenzo's face:
The guerdon of their murder they had got,
   And so left Florence in a moment's space,
Never to turn again. Away they went,
480 With blood upon their heads, to banishment.

LXI

O Melancholy, turn thine eyes away!
   O Music, Music, breathe despondingly!
O Echo, Echo, on some other day,
   From isles Lethean, sigh to us – O sigh!
485 Spirits of grief, sing not your 'Well-a-way!'
   For Isabel, sweet Isabel, will die –
Will die a death too lone and incomplete,
Now they have ta'en away her basil sweet.

LXII

Piteous she looked on dead and senseless things,
490   Asking for her lost basil amorously;
And with melodious chuckle in the strings
    Of her lorn voice, she oftentimes would cry
After the pilgrim in his wanderings,
    To ask him where her basil was, and why
495 'Twas hid from her: 'For cruel 'tis,' said she,
'To steal my basil-pot away from me.'

LXIII

And so she pined, and so she died forlorn,
    Imploring for her basil to the last.
No heart was there in Florence but did mourn
500   In pity of her love, so overcast.
And a sad ditty on this story born
    From mouth to mouth through all the country
        passed:
Still is the burthen sung – 'O cruelty,
To steal my basil-pot away from me!'

Old Meg

Old Meg she was a gipsy,
    And lived upon the moors,
Her bed it was the brown heath turf,
    And her house was out of doors.

5 Her apples were swart blackberries,
    Her currants pods o'broom,
Her wine was dew o'the wild white rose,
    Her book a churchyard tomb.

Her brothers were the craggy hills,
10   Her sisters larchen trees –
Alone with her great family
    She lived as she did please.

No breakfast had she many a morn,
    No dinner many a noon,
15   And 'stead of supper she would stare
    Full hard against the moon.

But every morn of woodbine fresh
    She made her garlanding,
And every night the dark glen yew
20   She wove, and she would sing.

And with her fingers old and brown,
    She plaited mats o'rushes,
And gave them to the cottagers
    She met among the bushes.

25   Old Meg was brave as Margaret Queen
    And tall as Amazon,
An old red blanket cloak she wore,
    A chip-hat had she on.
God rest her agèd bones somewhere –
30   She died full long agone!

Hyperion
A Fragment

Book I
Deep in the shady sadness of a vale
Far sunken from the healthy breath of morn,
Far from the fiery noon, and eve's one star,
Sat grey-haired Saturn, quiet as a stone,
5   Still as the silence round about his lair;
Forest on forest clung above his head
Like cloud on cloud. No stir of air was there,
Not so much life as on a summer's day
Robs not one light seed from the feathered grass,
10 But where the dead leaf fell, there did it rest.
A stream went voiceless by, still deadened more
By reason of his fallen divinity
Spreading a shade: the Naiad 'mid her reeds
Pressed her cold finger closer to her lips.

15   Along the margin-sand large foot-marks went,
No further than to where his feet had strayed,
And slept there since. Upon the sodden ground
His old right hand lay nerveless, listless, dead,
Unsceptred; and his realmless eyes were closed;
20 While his bowed head seemed listening to the Earth,
His ancient mother, for some comfort yet.

    It seemed no force could wake him from his place;
But there came one, who with a kindred hand
Touched his wide shoulders, after bending low
25 With reverence, though to one who knew it not.
She was a Goddess of the infant world;
By her in stature the tall Amazon
Had stood a pigmy's height: she would have ta'en

Achilles by the hair and bent his neck;
30 Or with a finger stayed Ixion's wheel.
Her face was large as that of Memphian sphinx,
Pedestalled haply in a palace court,
When sages looked to Egypt for their lore.
But O! how unlike marble was that face,
35 How beautiful, if sorrow had not made
Sorrow more beautiful than Beauty's self.
There was a listening fear in her regard,
As if calamity had begun;
As if the vanward clouds of evil days
40 Had spent their malice, and the sudden rear
Was with its storèd thunder labouring up.
One hand she pressed upon that aching spot
Where beats the human heart, as if just there,
Though an immortal, she felt cruel pain;
45 The other upon Saturn's bended neck
She laid, and to the level of his ear
Leaning with parted lips, some words she spake
In solemn tenor and deep organ tone –
Some mourning words, which in our feeble tongue
50 Would come in these like accents (O how frail
To that large utterance of the early Gods!)
'Saturn, look up! – though wherefore, poor old King?
I have no comfort for thee, no, not one:
I cannot say, "O wherefore sleepest thou?"
55 For heaven is parted from thee, and the earth
Knows thee not, thus afflicted, for a God;
And ocean too, with all its solemn noise,
Has from thy sceptre passed; and all the air
Is emptied of thine hoary majesty.
60 Thy thunder, conscious of the new command,
Rumbles reluctant o'er our fallen house;
And thy sharp lightning in unpractised hands

Scorches and burns our once serene domain.
O aching time! O moments big as years!
65 All as ye pass swell out the monstrous truth,
And press it so upon our weary griefs
That unbelief has not a space to breathe.
Saturn, sleep on – O thoughtless, why did I
Thus violate thy slumbrous solitude?
70 Why should I ope thy melancholy eyes?
Saturn, sleep on, while at thy feet I weep!'

As when, upon a trancèd summer-night,
Those green-robed senators of mighty woods,
Tall oaks, branch-charmèd by the earnest stars,
75 Dream, and so dream all night without a stir,
Save from one gradual solitary gust
Which comes upon the silence, and dies off,
As if the ebbing air had but one wave;
So came these words and went; the while in tears
80 She touched her fair large forehead to the ground,
Just where her falling hair might be outspread
A soft and silken mat for Saturn's feet.
One moon, with alteration slow, had shed
Her silver seasons four upon the night,
85 And still these two were postured motionless,
Like natural sculpture in cathedral cavern;
The frozen God still couchant on the earth,
And the sad Goddess weeping at his feet:
Until at length old Saturn lifted up
90 His faded eyes, and saw his kingdom gone,
And all the gloom and sorrow of the place,
And that fair kneeling Goddess; and then spake,
As with a palsied tongue, and while his beard
Shook horrid with such aspen-malady:
95 'O tender spouse of gold Hyperion,

Thea, I feel thee ere I see thy face;
Look up, and let me see our doom in it;
Look up, and tell me if this feeble shape
Is Saturn's; tell me, if thou hear'st the voice
100 Of Saturn; tell me, if this wrinkling brow,
Naked and bare of its great diadem,
Peers like the front of Saturn. Who had power
To make me desolate? whence came the strength?
How was it nurtured to such bursting forth,
105 While Fate seemed strangled in my nervous grasp?
But it is so; and I am smothered up,
And buried from all godlike exercise
Of influence benign on planets pale,
Of admonitions to the winds and seas,
110 Of peaceful sway above man's harvesting,
And all those acts which Deity supreme
Doth ease its heart of love in. – I am gone
Away from my own bosom; I have left
My strong identity, my real self,
115 Somewhere between the throne and where I sit
Here on this spot of earth. Search, Thea, search!
Open thine eyes eterne, and sphere them round
Upon all space – space starred, and lorn of light;
Space regioned with life-air; and barren void;
120 Spaces of fire, and all the yawn of hell.
Search, Thea, search! and tell me, if thou seest
A certain shape or shadow, making way
With wings or chariot fierce to repossess
A heaven he lost erewhile: it must – it must
125 Be of ripe progress: Saturn must be King.
Yes, there must be a golden victory;
There must be Gods thrown down, and trumpets
blown
Of triumph calm, and hymns of festival

Upon the gold clouds metropolitan,
130 Voices of soft proclaim, and silver stir
Of strings in hollow shells; and there shall be
Beautiful things made new, for the surprise
Of the sky-children. I will give command:
Thea! Thea! Thea! where is Saturn?'

135   This passion lifted him upon his feet,
And made his hands to struggle in the air,
His Druid locks to shake and ooze with sweat,
His eyes to fever out, his voice to cease.
He stood, and heard not Thea's sobbing deep;
140 A little time, and then again he snatched
Utterance thus: 'But cannot I create?
Cannot I form? Cannot I fashion forth
Another world, another universe,
To overbear and crumble this to naught?
145 Where is another Chaos? Where?' – That word
Found way unto Olympus, and made quake
The rebel three. Thea was startled up,
And in her bearing was a sort of hope,
As thus she quick-voiced spake, yet full of awe.

150   'This cheers our fallen house: come to our friends,
O Saturn! come away, and give them heart.
I know the covert, for thence came I hither.'
Thus brief; then with beseeching eyes she went
With backward footing through the shade a space:
155 He followed, and she turned to lead the way
Through agèd boughs, that yielded like the mist
Which eagles cleave up-mounting from their nest.

Meanwhile in other realms big tears were shed,
More sorrow like to this, and such like woe,

49

160   Too huge for mortal tongue or pen of scribe.
        The Titans fierce, self-hid, or prison-bound,
        Groaned for the old allegiance once more,
        And listened in sharp pain for Saturn's voice.
        But one of the whole mammoth-brood still kept
165   His sovereignty, and rule, and majesty –
        Blazing Hyperion on his orbèd fire
        Still sat, still snuffed the incense, teeming up
        From man to the sun's God; yet unsecure:
        For as among us mortals omens drear
170   Fright and perplex, so also shuddered he –
        Not at dog's howl, or gloom-bird's hated screech,
        Or the familiar visiting of one
        Upon the first toll of his passing-bell,
        Or prophesyings of the midnight lamp;
175   But horrors, portioned to a giant nerve,
        Oft made Hyperion ache. His palace bright
        Bastioned with pyramids of glowing gold,
        And touched with shade of bronzèd obelisks,
        Glared a blood-red through all its thousand courts,
180   Arches, and domes, and fiery galleries;
        And all its curtains of Aurorian clouds
        Flushed angerly, while sometimes eagle's wings,
        Unseen before by Gods or wondering men,
        Darkened the place, and neighing steeds were heard,
185   Not heard before by Gods or wondering men.
        Also, when he would taste the spicy wreaths
        Of incense, breathed aloft from sacred hills,
        Instead of sweets, his ample palate took
        Savour of poisonous brass and metal sick:
190   And so, when harboured in the sleepy west,
        After the full completion of fair day,
        For rest divine upon exalted couch
        And slumber in the arms of melody,

He paced away the pleasant hours of ease
195 With stride colossal, on from hall to hall;
While far within each aisle and deep recess,
His wingèd minions in close clusters stood,
Amazed and full of fear; like anxious men
Who on wide plains gather in panting troops,
200 When earthquakes jar their battlements and towers.
Even now, while Saturn, roused from icy trance,
Went step for step with Thea through the woods,
Hyperion, leaving twilight in the rear,
Came slope upon the threshold of the west;
205 Then, as he was wont, his palace-door flew ope
In smoothest silence, save what solemn tubes,
Blown by the serious Zephyrs, gave of sweet
And wandering sounds, slow-breathèd melodies –
And like a rose in vermeil tint and shape,
210 In fragrance soft, and coolness to the eye,
That inlet to severe magnificence
Stood full blown, for the God to enter in.

He entered, but he entered full of wrath;
His flaming robes streamed out beyond his heels,
215 And gave a roar, as if of earthly fire,
That scared away the meek ethereal Hours
And made their dove-wings tremble. On he flared,
From stately nave to nave, from vault to vault,
Through bowers of fragrant and enwreathèd light,
220 And diamond-pavèd lustrous long arcades,
Until he reached the great main cupola.
There standing fierce beneath, he stamped his foot,
And from the basement deep to the high towers
Jarred his own golden region; and before
225 The quavering thunder thereupon had ceased,
His voice leapt out, despite of god-like curb,

To this result: 'O dreams of day and night!
O monstrous forms! O effigies of pain!
O spectres busy in a cold, cold gloom!
230   O lank-eared Phantoms of black-weeded pools!
Why do I know ye? Why have I seen ye? Why
Is my eternal essence thus distraught
To see and to behold these horrors new?
Saturn is fallen, am I too to fall?
235   Am I to leave this haven of my rest,
This cradle of my glory, this soft clime,
This calm luxuriance of blissful light,
These crystalline pavilions, and pure fanes,
Of all my lucent empire? It is left
240   Deserted, void, nor any haunt of mine.
The blaze, the splendour, and the symmetry,
I cannot see – but darkness, death and darkness.
Even here, into my centre of repose,
The shady visions come to domineer,
245   Insult, and blind, and stifle up my pomp. –
Fall! – No, by Tellus and her briny robes!
Over the fiery frontier of my realms
I will advance a terrible right arm
Shall scare that infant thunderer, rebel Jove,
250   And bid old Saturn take his throne again.' –
He spake, and ceased, the while a heavier threat
Held struggle with his throat but came not forth;
For as in theatres of crowded men
Hubbub increases more they call out 'Hush!',
255   So at Hyperion's words the Phantoms pale
Bestirred themselves, thrice horrible and cold;
And from the mirrored level where he stood
A mist arose, as from a scummy marsh.
At this, through all his bulk an agony
260   Crept gradual, from the feet unto the crown,

Like a lithe serpent vast and muscular
Making slow way, with head and neck convulsed
From over-strainèd might. Released, he fled
To the eastern gates, and full six dewy hours
265   Before the dawn in season due should blush,
He breathed fierce breath against the sleepy portals,
Cleared them of heavy vapours, burst them wide
Suddenly on the ocean's chilly streams.
The planet orb of fire, whereon he rode
270   Each day from east to west the heaven through,
Spun round in sable curtaining of clouds;
Not therefore veilèd quite, blindfold, and hid,
But ever and anon the glancing spheres,
Circles, and arcs, and broad-belting colure,
275   Glowed through, and wrought upon the muffling dark
Sweet-shapèd lightnings from the nadir deep
Up to the zenith – hieroglyphics old
Which sages and keen-eyed astrologers
Then living on the earth, with labouring thought
280   Won from the gaze of many centuries –
Now lost, save what we find on remnants huge
Of stone, or marble swart, their import gone,
Their wisdom long since fled. Two wings this orb
Possessed for glory, two fair argent wings,
285   Ever exalted at the God's approach:
And now, from forth the gloom their plumes immense
Rose, one by one, till all outspreaded were;
While still the dazzling globe maintained eclipse,
Awaiting for Hyperion's command.
290   Fain would he have commanded, fain took throne
And bid the day begin, if but for change.
He might not. – No, though a primeval God:
The sacred seasons might not be disturbed.
Therefore the operations of the dawn

295   Stayed in their birth, even as here 'tis told.
       Those silver wings expanded sisterly,
       Eager to sail their orb; the porches wide
       Opened upon the dusk demesnes of night;
       And the bright Titan, frenzied with new woes,
300   Unused to bend, by hard compulsion bent
       His spirit to the sorrow of the time;
       And all along a dismal rack of clouds,
       Upon the boundaries of day and night,
       He stretched himself in grief and radiance faint.
305   There as he lay, the Heaven with its stars
       Looked down on him with pity, and the voice
       Of Coelus, from the universal space,
       Thus whispered low and solemn in his ear:
       'O brightest of my children dear, earth-born
310   And sky-engendered, Son of Mysteries
       All unrevealèd even to the powers
       Which met at thy creating; at whose joys
       And palpitations sweet, and pleasures soft,
       I, Coelus, wonder how they came and whence;
315   And at the fruits thereof what shapes they be,
       Distinct, and visible – symbols divine,
       Manifestations of that beauteous life
       Diffused unseen throughout eternal space:
       Of these new-formed art thou, O brightest child!
320   Of these, thy brethren and the Goddesses!
       There is sad feud among ye, and rebellion
       Of son against his sire. I saw him fall,
       I saw my first-born tumbled from his throne!
       To me his arms were spread, to me his voice
325   Found way from forth the thunders round his head!
       Pale wox I, and in vapours hid my face.
       Art thou, too, near such doom? Vague fear there is:
       For I have seen my sons most unlike Gods.

Divine ye were created, and divine
330   In sad demeanour, solemn, undisturbed,
Unrufflèd, like high Gods, ye lived and ruled:
Now I behold in you fear, hope, and wrath;
Actions of rage and passion – even as
I see them, on the mortal world beneath,
335   In men who die. This is the grief, O Son!
Sad sign of ruin, sudden dismay, and fall!
Yet do not strive; as thou art capable,
As thou canst move about, an evident God;
And canst oppose to each malignant hour
340   Ethereal presence. I am but a voice;
My life is but the life of winds and tides,
No more than winds and tides can avail. –
But thou canst. – Be thou therefore in the van
Of circumstance; yea, seize the arrow's barb
345   Before the tense string murmur. – To the earth!
For there thou wilt find Saturn, and his woes.
Meantime I will keep watch on thy bright sun,
And of thy seasons be a careful nurse.' –
Ere half this region-whisper had come down,
350   Hyperion arose, and on the stars
Lifted his curvèd lids, and kept them wide
Until it ceased; and still he kept them wide;
And still they were the same bright, patient stars.
Then with a slow incline of his broad breast,
355   Like to a diver in the pearly seas,
Forward he stooped over the airy shore,
And plunged all noiseless into the deep night.

Book II
Just at the self-same beat of Time's wide wings,
Hyperion slid into the rustled air
And Saturn gained with Thea that sad place

Where Cybele and the bruised Titans mourned.
5   It was a den where no insulting light
Could glimmer on their tears; where their own groans
They felt, but heard not, for the solid roar
Of thunderous waterfalls and torrents hoarse,
Pouring a constant bulk, uncertain where.
10   Crag jutting forth to crag, and rocks that seemed
Ever as if just rising from a sleep,
Forehead to forehead held their monstrous horns;
And thus in thousand hugest fantasies
Made a fit roofing to this nest of woe.
15   Instead of thrones, hard flint they sat upon,
Couches of rugged stone, and slaty ridge
Stubborned with iron. All were not assembled:
Some chained in torture, and some wandering.
Coeus, and Gyges, and Briareüs,
20   Typhon, and Dolor, and Porphyrion,
With many more, the brawniest in assault,
Were pent in regions of laborious breath;
Dungeoned in opaque element, to keep
Their clenchèd teeth still clenched, and all their limbs
25   Locked up like veins of metal, cramped and screwed;
Without a motion, save of their big hearts
Heaving in pain, and horribly convulsed
With sanguine fev'rous boiling gurge of pulse.
Mnemosyne was straying in the world;
30   Far from her moon had Phoebe wanderèd;
And many else were free to roam abroad,
But for the main, here found they covert drear.
Scarce images of life, one here, one there,
Lay vast and edgeways; like a dismal cirque
35   Of Druid stones, upon a forlorn moor,
When the chill rain begins at shut of eve,
In dull November, and their chancel vault,

The Heaven itself, is blinded throughout night.
Each one kept shroud, nor to his neighbour gave
40 Or word, or look, or action of despair.
Creüs was one; his ponderous iron mace
Lay by him, and a shattered rib of rock
Told of his rage, ere he thus sank and pined.
Iäpetus another; in his grasp,
45 A serpent's plashy neck; its barbèd tongue
Squeezed from the gorge, and all its uncurled length
Dead – and because the creature could not spit
Its poison in the eyes of conquering Jove.
Next Cottus; prone he lay, chin uppermost,
50 As though in pain, for still upon the flint
He ground severe his skull, with open mouth
And eyes at horrid working. Nearest him
Asia, born of most enormous Caf,
Who cost her mother Tellus keener pangs,
55 Though feminine, than any of her sons:
More thought than woe was in her dusky face,
For she was prophesying of her glory;
And in her wide imagination stood
Palm-shaded temples, and high rival fanes,
60 By Oxus or in Ganges' sacred isles.
Even as Hope upon her anchor leans,
So leant she, not so fair, upon a tusk
Shed from the broadest of her elephants.
Above her, on a crag's uneasy shelve,
65 Upon his elbow raised, all prostrate else,
Shadowed Enceladus – once tame and mild
As grazing ox unworried in the meads;
Now tiger-passioned, lion-thoughted, wroth,
He meditated, plotted, and even now
70 Was hurling mountains in that second war,
Not long delayed, that scared the younger Gods

To hide themselves in forms of beast and bird.
Not far hence Atlas; and beside him prone
Phorcus, the sire of Gorgons. Neighboured close

75   Oceanus, and Tethys, in whose lap
Sobbed Clymene among her tangled hair.
In midst of all lay Themis, at the feet
Of Ops the queen all clouded round from sight;
No shape distinguishable, more than when

80   Thick night confounds the pine-tops with the clouds –
And many else whose names may not be told.
For when the Muse's wings are air-ward spread,
Who shall delay her flight? And she must chant
Of Saturn, and his guide, who now had climbed

85   With damp and slippery footing from a depth
More horrid still. Above a sombre cliff
Their heads appeared, and up their stature grew
Till on the level height their steps found ease:
Then Thea spread abroad her trembling arms

90   Upon the precincts of this nest of pain,
And sidelong fixed her eye on Saturn's face.
There saw she direst strife – the supreme God
At war with all the frailty of grief,
Of rage, of fear, anxiety, revenge,

95   Remorse, spleen, hope, but most of all despair.
Against these plagues he strove in vain; for Fate
Had poured a mortal oil upon his head,
A disanointing poison, so that Thea,
Affrighted, kept her still, and let him pass

100   First onwards in, among the fallen tribe.

    As with us mortal men, the laden heart
Is persecuted more, and fevered more,
When it is nighing to the mournful house
Where other hearts are sick of the same bruise;

105 So Saturn, as he walked into the midst,
Felt faint, and would have sunk among the rest,
But that he met Enceladus's eye,
Whose mightiness, and awe of him, at once
Came like an inspiration; and he shouted,
110 'Titans, behold your God!' At which some groaned;
Some started on their feet; some also shouted;
Some wept, some wailed, all bowed with reverence;
And Ops, uplifting her black folded veil,
Showed her pale cheeks, and all her forehead wan,
115 Her eye-brows thin and jet, and hollow eyes.
There is a roaring in the bleak-grown pines
When Winter lifts his voice; there is a noise
Among immortals when a God gives sign,
With hushing finger, how he means to load
120 His tongue with the full weight of utterless thought,
With thunder, and with music, and with pomp:
Such noise is as the roar of bleak-grown pines,
Which, when it ceases in this mountained world,
No other sound succeeds; but ceasing here,
125 Among these fallen, Saturn's voice therefrom
Grew up like organ, that begins anew
Its strain, when other harmonies, stopped short,
Leave the dinned air vibrating silverly.
Thus grew it up: 'Not in my own sad breast,
130 Which is its own great judge and searcher-out,
Can I find reasons why ye should be thus:
Not in the legend of the first of days,
Studied from that old spirit-leavèd book
Which starry Uranus with finger bright
135 Saved from the shores of darkness, when the waves
Low-ebbed still hid it up in shallow gloom –
And the which book ye know I ever kept
For my firm-basèd footstool – Ah, infirm!

Not there, nor in sign, symbol, or portent
140 Of element, earth, water, air, and fire –
At war, at peace, or inter-quarrelling
One against one, or two, or three, or all
Each several one against the other three,
As fire with air loud warring when rain-floods
145 Drown both, and press them both against earth's face,
Where, finding sulphur, a quadruple wrath
Unhinges the poor world – not in that strife,
Wherefrom I take strange lore, and read it deep,
Can I find reason why ye should be thus –
150 No, nowhere can unriddle, though I search,
And pore on Nature's universal scroll
Even to swooning, why ye, Divinities,
The first-born of all shaped and palpable Gods,
Should cower beneath what, in comparison,
155 Is untremendous might. Yet ye are here,
O'erwhelmed, and spurned, and battered, ye are here!
O Titans, shall I say, "Arise!"? – Ye groan:
Shall I say "Crouch!"? – Ye groan. What can I then?
O Heaven wide! O unseen parent dear!
160 What can I? Tell me, all ye brethren Gods,
How we can war, how engine our great wrath!
O speak your counsel now, for Saturn's ear
Is all a-hungered. Thou, Oceanus,
Ponderest high and deep, and in thy face
165 I see, astonied, that severe content
Which comes of thought and musing. Give us help!'

So ended Saturn; and the God of the Sea,
Sophist and sage from no Athenian grove,
But cogitation in his watery shades,
170 Arose, with locks not oozy, and began,
In murmurs which his first-endeavouring tongue

Caught infant-like from the far-foamèd sands.
'O ye, whom wrath consumes! who, passion-stung,
Writhe at defeat, and nurse your agonies!
175 Shut up your senses, stifle up your ears,
My voice is not a bellows unto ire.
Yet listen, ye who will, whilst I bring proof
How ye, perforce, must be content to stoop;
And in the proof much comfort will I give,
180 If ye will take that comfort in its truth.
We fall by course of Nature's law, not force
Of thunder, or of Jove. Great Saturn, thou
Hast sifted well the atom-universe;
But for this reason, that thou art the King,
185 And only blind from sheer supremacy,
One avenue was shaded from thine eyes,
Through which I wandered to eternal truth.
And first, as thou wast not the first of powers,
So art thou not the last; it cannot be:
190 Thou art not the beginning nor the end.
From Chaos and parental Darkness came
Light, the first fruits of that intestine broil,
That sullen ferment, which for wondrous ends
Was ripening in itself. The ripe hour came,
195 And with it Light, and Light, engendering
Upon its own producer, forthwith touched
The whole enormous matter into life.
Upon that very hour, our parentage,
The Heavens, and the Earth, were manifest:
200 Then thou first born, and we the giant race,
Found ourselves ruling new and beauteous realms.
Now comes the pain of truth, to whom 'tis pain –
O folly! for to bear all naked truths,
And to envisage circumstance, all calm,
205 That is the top of sovereignty. Mark well!

As Heaven and Earth are fairer, fairer far
Than Chaos and blank Darkness, though once chiefs;
And as we show beyond that Heaven and Earth
In form and shape compact and beautiful,
210 In will, in action free, companionship,
And thousand other signs of purer life;
So on our heels a fresh perfection treads,
A power more strong in beauty, born of us
And fated to excel us, as we pass
215 In glory that old Darkness: nor are we
Thereby more conquered, than by us the rule
Of shapeless Chaos. Say, doth the dull soil
Quarrel with the proud forests it hath fed,
And feedeth still, more comely than itself?
220 Can it deny the chiefdom of green groves?
Or shall the tree be envious of the dove
Because it cooeth, and hath snowy wings
To wander wherewithal and find its joys?
We are such forest-trees, and our fair boughs
225 Have bred forth, not pale solitary doves,
But eagles golden-feathered, who do tower
Above us in their beauty, and must reign
In right thereof. For 'tis the eternal law
That first in beauty should be first in might.
230 Yea, by that law, another race may drive
Our conquerors to mourn as we do now.
Have ye beheld the young God of the Seas,
My dispossessor? Have ye seen his face?
Have ye beheld his chariot, foamed along
235 By noble wingèd creatures he hath made?
I saw him on the calmèd waters scud,
With such a glow of beauty in his eyes,
That it enforced me to bid sad farewell
To all my empire: farewell sad I took,

240   And hither came, to see how dolorous fate
        Had wrought upon ye; and how I might best
        Give consolation in this woe extreme.
        Receive the truth, and let it be your balm.'

        Whether through posed conviction, or disdain,
245   They guarded silence, when Oceanus
        Left murmuring, what deepest thought can tell?
        But so it was; none answered for a space,
        Save one whom none regarded, Clymene;
        And yet she answered not, only complained,
250   With hectic lips, and eyes up-looking mild,
        Thus wording timidly among the fierce:
        'O Father, I am here the simplest voice,
        And all my knowledge is that joy is gone,
        And this thing woe crept in among our hearts,
255   There to remain for ever, as I fear.
        I would not bode of evil, if I thought
        So weak a creature could turn off the help
        Which by just right should come of mighty Gods;
        Yet let me tell my sorrow, let me tell
260   Of what I heard, and how it made me weep,
        And know that we had parted from all hope.
        I stood upon a shore, a pleasant shore,
        Where a sweet clime was breathèd from a land
        Of fragrance, quietness, and trees, and flowers.
265   Full of calm joy it was, as I of grief;
        Too full of joy and soft delicious warmth;
        So that I felt a movement in my heart
        To chide, and to reproach that solitude
        With songs of misery, music of our woes;
270   And sat me down, and took a mouthèd shell
        And murmured into it, and made melody –
        O melody no more! for while I sang,

And with poor skill let pass into the breeze
The dull shell's echo, from a bowery strand
275 Just opposite, an island of the sea,
There came enchantment with the shifting wind,
That did both drown and keep alive my ears.
I threw my shell away upon the sand,
And a wave filled it, as my sense was filled
280 With that new blissful golden melody.
A living death was in each gush of sounds,
Each family of rapturous hurried notes,
That fell, one after one, yet all at once,
Like pearl beads dropping sudden from their string;
285 And then another, then another strain,
Each like a dove leaving its olive perch,
With music winged instead of silent plumes,
To hover round my head, and make me sick
Of joy and grief at once. Grief overcame,
290 And I was stopping up my frantic ears,
When, past all hindrance of my trembling hands,
A voice came sweeter, sweeter than all tune,
And still it cried, "Apollo! young Apollo!
The morning-bright Apollo! young Apollo!"
295 I fled, it followed me, and cried "Apollo!"
O Father, and O Brethren, had ye felt
Those pains of mine – O Saturn, hadst thou felt,
Ye would not call this too indulgèd tongue
Presumptuous, in thus venturing to be heard.'

300   So far her voice flowed on, like timorous brook
That, lingering along a pebbled coast,
Doth fear to meet the sea: but sea it met,
And shuddered; for the overwhelming voice
Of huge Enceladus swallowed it in wrath:
305 The ponderous syllables, like sullen waves

In the half-glutted hollows of reef-rocks,
Came booming thus, while still upon his arm
He leaned – not rising, from supreme contempt:
'Or shall we listen to the over-wise,
310 Or to the over-foolish, Giant-Gods?
Not thunderbolt on thunderbolt, till all
That rebel Jove's whole armoury were spent,
Not world on world upon these shoulders piled
Could agonize me more than baby-words
315 In midst of this dethronement horrible.
Speak! Roar! Shout! Yell! ye sleepy Titans all.
Do ye forget the blows, the buffets vile?
Are ye not smitten by a youngling arm?
Dost thou forget, sham Monarch of the Waves,
320 Thy scalding in the seas? What, have I roused
Your spleens with so few simple words as these?
O joy! for now I see ye are not lost:
O joy! for now I see a thousand eyes
Wide-glaring for revenge!' – As this he said,
325 He lifted up his stature vast, and stood,
Still without intermission speaking thus:
'Now ye are flames, I'll tell you how to burn,
And purge the ether of our enemies;
How to feed fierce the crooked stings of fire,
330 And singe away the swollen clouds of Jove,
Stifling that puny essence in its tent.
O let him feel the evil he hath done;
For though I scorn Oceanus's lore,
Much pain have I for more than loss of realms:
335 The days of peace and slumbrous calm are fled;
Those days, all innocent of scathing war,
When all the fair Existences of heaven
Came open-eyed to guess what we would speak –
That was before our brows were taught to frown,

340   Before our lips knew else but solemn sounds;
      That was before we knew the wingèd thing,
      Victory, might be lost, or might be won.
      And be ye mindful that Hyperion,
      Our brightest brother, still is undisgraced –
345   Hyperion, lo! his radiance is here!'

          All eyes were on Enceladus's face,
      And they beheld, while still Hyperion's name
      Flew from his lips up to the vaulted rocks,
      A pallid gleam across his features stern –
350   Not savage, for he saw full many a God
      Wroth as himself. He looked upon them all,
      And in each face he saw a gleam of light,
      But splendider in Saturn's, whose hoar locks
      Shone like the bubbling foam about a keel
355   When the prow sweeps into a midnight cove.
      In pale and silver silence they remained,
      Till suddenly a splendour, like the morn,
      Pervaded all the beetling gloomy steeps,
      All the sad spaces of oblivion,
360   And every gulf, and every chasm old,
      And every height, and every sullen depth,
      Voiceless, or hoarse with loud tormented streams;
      And all the everlasting cataracts,
      And all the headlong torrents far and near,
365   Mantled before in darkness and huge shade,
      Now saw the light and made it terrible.
      It was Hyperion: a granite peak
      His bright feet touched, and there he stayed to view
      The misery his brilliance had betrayed
370   To the most hateful seeing of itself.
      Golden his hair of short Numidian curl,
      Regal his shape majestic, a vast shade

In midst of his own brightness, like the bulk
Of Memnon's image at the set of sun
375 To one who travels from the dusking East:
Sighs, too, as mournful as that Memnon's harp,
He uttered, while his hands contemplative
He pressed together, and in silence stood.
Despondence seized again the fallen Gods
380 At sight of the dejected King of Day,
And many hid their faces from the light:
But fierce Enceladus sent forth his eyes
Among the brotherhood; and, at their glare,
Uprose Iäpetus, and Creüs too,
385 And Phorcus, sea-born, and together strode
To where he towered on his eminence.
There those four shouted forth old Saturn's name;
Hyperion from the peak loud answered, 'Saturn!'
Saturn sat near the Mother of the Gods,
390 In whose face was no joy, though all the Gods
Gave from their hollow throats the name of 'Saturn!'

Book III
Thus in alternate uproar and sad peace,
Amazèd were those Titans utterly.
O leave them, Muse! O leave them to their woes;
For thou art weak to sing such tumults dire:
5 A solitary sorrow best befits
Thy lips, and antheming a lonely grief.
Leave them, O Muse! for thou anon wilt find
Many a fallen old Divinity
Wandering in vain about bewildered shores.
10 Meantime touch piously the Delphic harp,
And not a wind of heaven but will breathe
In aid soft warble from the Dorian flute;
For lo! 'tis for the Father of all verse.

Flush every thing that hath a vermeil hue,
15   Let the rose glow intense and warm the air,
And let the clouds of even and of morn
Float in voluptuous fleeces o'er the hills;
Let the red wine within the goblet boil,
Cold as a bubbling well; let faint-lipped shells,
20   On sands, or in great deeps, vermilion turn
Through all their labyrinths; and let the maid
Blush keenly, as with some warm kiss surprised.
Chief isle of the embowered Cyclades,
Rejoice, O Delos, with thine olives green,
25   And poplars, and lawn-shading palms, and beech,
In which the Zephyr breathes the loudest song,
And hazels thick, dark-stemmed beneath the shade:
Apollo is once more the golden theme!
Where was he, when the Giant of the Sun
30   Stood bright, amid the sorrow of his peers?
Together had he left his mother fair
And his twin-sister sleeping in their bower,
And in the morning twilight wandered forth
Beside the osiers of a rivulet,
35   Full ankle-deep in lilies of the vale.
The nightingale had ceased, and a few stars
Were lingering in the heavens, while the thrush
Began calm-throated. Throughout all the isle
There was no covert, no retirèd cave
40   Unhaunted by the murmurous noise of waves,
Though scarcely heard in many a green recess.
He listened, and he wept, and his bright tears
Went trickling down the golden bow he held.
Thus with half-shut suffusèd eyes he stood,
45   While from beneath some cumbrous boughs hard by
With solemn step an awful Goddess came,
And there was purport in her looks for him,

Which he with eager guess began to read
Perplexed, the while melodiously he said:
50 'How cam'st thou over the unfooted sea?
Or hath that antique mien and robèd form
Moved in these vales invisible till now?
Sure I have heard those vestments sweeping o'er
The fallen leaves, when I have sat alone
55 In cool mid-forest. Surely I have traced
The rustle of those ample skirts about
These grassy solitudes, and seen the flowers
Lift up their heads, as still the whisper passed.
Goddess! I have beheld those eyes before,
60 And their eternal calm, and all that face,
Or I have dreamed.' – 'Yes,' said the supreme shape,
Thou hast dreamed of me; and awaking up
Didst find a lyre all golden by thy side,
Whose strings touched by thy fingers, all the vast
65 Unwearied ear of the whole universe
Listened in pain and pleasure at the birth
Of such new tuneful wonder. Is't not strange
That thou shouldst weep, so gifted? Tell me, youth,
What sorrow thou canst feel; for I am sad
70 When thou dost shed a tear. Explain thy griefs
To one who in this lonely isle hath been
The watcher of thy sleep and hours of life,
From the young day when first thy infant hand
Plucked witless the weak flowers, till thine arm
75 Could bend that bow heroic to all times.
Show thy heart's secret to an ancient Power
Who hath forsaken old and sacred thrones
For prophecies of thee, and for the sake
Of loveliness new born.' – Apollo then,
80 With sudden scrutiny and gloomless eyes,
Thus answered, while his white melodious throat

Throbbed with the syllables: 'Mnemosyne!
Thy name is on my tongue, I know not how;
Why should I tell thee what thou so well seest?
85   Why should I strive to show what from thy lips
Would come to no mystery? For me, dark, dark,
And painful vile oblivion seals my eyes:
I strive to search wherefore I am so sad,
Until a melancholy numbs my limbs;
90   And then upon the grass I sit, and moan,
Like one who once had wings. O why should I
Feel cursed and thwarted, when the liegeless air
Yields to my step aspirant? Why should I
Spurn the green turf as hateful to my feet?
95   Goddess benign, point forth some unknown thing:
Are there not other regions than this isle?
What are the stars? There is the sun, the sun!
And the most patient brilliance of the moon!
And stars by thousands! Point me out the way
100   To any one particular beauteous star,
And I will flit into it with my lyre,
And make its silvery splendour pant with bliss.
I have heard the cloudy thunder. Where is power?
Whose hand, whose essence, what Divinity
105   Makes this alarum in the elements,
While I here idle listen on the shores
In fearless yet in aching ignorance?
O tell me, lonely Goddess, by thy harp,
That waileth every morn and eventide,
110   Tell me why thus I rave, about these groves!
Mute thou remainest – mute! yet I can read
A wondrous lesson in thy silent face:
Knowledge enormous makes a God of me.
Names, deeds, grey legends, dire events, rebellions,
115   Majesties, sovran voices, agonies,

Creations and destroying, all at once
Pour into the wide hollows of my brain,
And deify me, as if some blithe wine
Or bright elixir peerless I had drunk,
120 And so become immortal.' – Thus the God,
While his enkindlèd eyes, with level glance
Beneath his white soft temples, steadfast kept
Trembling with light upon Mnemosyne.
Soon wild commotions shook him, and made flush
125 All the immortal fairness of his limbs –
Most like the struggle at the gate of death;
Or liker still to one who should take leave
Of pale immortal death, and with a pang
As hot as death's is chill, with fierce convulse
130 Die into life: so young Apollo anguished.
His very hair, his golden tresses famed
Kept undulation round his eager neck.
During the pain Mnemosyne upheld
Her arms as one who prophesied. – At length
135 Apollo shrieked – and lo! from all his limbs
Celestial...

Ode

Bards of Passion and of Mirth,
Ye have left your souls on earth!
Have ye souls in heaven too,
Double-lived in regions new?
5 Yes, and those of heaven commune
With the spheres of sun and moon;
With the noise of fountains wondrous,
And the parle of voices thund'rous;
With the whisper of heaven's trees

10 And one another, in soft ease
    Seated on Elysian lawns
    Browsed by none but Dian's fawns;
    Underneath large blue-bells tented,
    Where the daisies are rose-scented,
15 And the rose herself has got
    Perfume which on earth is not;
    Where the nightingale doth sing
    Not a senseless, trancèd thing,
    But divine melodious truth;
20 Philosophic numbers smooth;
    Tales and golden histories
    Of heaven and its mysteries.

        Thus ye live on high, and then
    On the earth ye live again;
25 And the souls ye left behind you
    Teach us, here, the way to find you,
    Where your other souls are joying,
    Never slumbered, never cloying.
    Here, your earth-born souls still speak
30 To mortals, of their little week;
    Of their sorrows and delights;
    Of their passions and their spites;
    Of their glory and their shame;
    What does strengthen and what maim.
35 Thus ye teach us, every day,
    Wisdom, though fled far away.

        Bards of Passion and of Mirth,
    Ye have left your souls on earth!
    Ye have souls in heaven too,
40 Double-lived in regions new!

Fancy

Ever let the Fancy roam,
Pleasure never is at home:
At a touch sweet Pleasure melteth,
Like to bubbles when rain pelteth.
5   Then let wingèd Fancy wander
Through the thought still spread beyond her:
Open wide the mind's cage-door,
She'll dart forth, and cloudward soar.
O sweet Fancy! let her loose –
10 Summer's joys are spoilt by use,
And the enjoying of the Spring
Fades as does its blossoming;
Autumn's red-lipped fruitage too,
Blushing through the mist and dew,
15 Cloys with tasting. What do then?
Sit thee by the ingle, when
The sear faggot blazes bright,
Spirit of a winter's night;
When the soundless earth is muffled,
20 And the cakèd snow is shuffled
From the ploughboy's heavy shoon;
When the Night doth meet the Noon
In a dark conspiracy
To banish Even from her sky.
25 Sit thee there, and send abroad,
With a mind self-overawed,
Fancy, high-commissioned – send her!
She has vassals to attend her:
She will bring, in spite of frost,
30 Beauties that the earth hath lost;
She will bring thee, all together,
All delights of summer weather;

All the buds and bells of May,
From dewy sward or thorny spray;
35   All the heapèd Autumn's wealth,
With a still, mysterious stealth:
She will mix these pleasures up
Like three fit wines in a cup,
And thou shalt quaff it – thou shalt hear
40   Distant harvest-carols clear;
Rustle of the reapèd corn;
Sweet birds antheming the morn:
And, in the same moment – hark!
'Tis the early April lark,
45   Or the rooks, with busy caw,
Foraging for sticks and straw.
Thou shalt, at one glance, behold
The daisy and the marigold;
White-plumed lilies, and the first
50   Hedge-grown primrose that hath burst;
Shaded hyacinth, alway
Sapphire queen of the mid-May;
And every leaf, and every flower
Pearlèd with the self-same shower.
55   Thou shalt see the field-mouse peep
Meagre from its cellèd sleep;
And the snake all winter-thin
Cast on sunny bank its skin;
Freckled nest-eggs thou shalt see
60   Hatching in the hawthorn-tree,
When the hen-bird's wing doth rest
Quiet on her mossy nest;
Then the hurry and alarm
When the bee-hive casts its swarm;
65   Acorns ripe down-pattering,
While the autumn breezes sing.

O, sweet Fancy! let her loose;
Every thing is spoilt by use:
Where's the cheek that doth not fade,
70   Too much gazed at? Where's the maid
Whose lip mature is ever new?
Where's the eye, however blue,
Doth not weary? Where's the face
One would meet in every place?
75   Where's the voice, however soft,
One would hear so very oft?
At a touch sweet Pleasure melteth
Like to bubbles when rain pelteth.
Let, then, wingèd Fancy find
80   Thee a mistress to thy mind:
Dulcet-eyed as Ceres' daughter,
Ere the God of Torment taught her
How to frown and how to chide;
With a waist and with a side
85   White as Hebe's, when her zone
Slipped its golden clasp, and down
Fell her kirtle to her feet,
While she held the goblet sweet,
And Jove grew languid. – Break the mesh
90   Of the Fancy's silken leash;
Quickly break her prison-string
And such joys as these she'll bring.
Let the wingèd Fancy roam,
Pleasure never is at home.

The Eve of St Agnes

I

St Agnes' Eve – Ah, bitter chill it was!
The owl, for all his feathers, was a-cold;
The hare limped trembling through the frozen grass,
And silent was the flock in woolly fold:
5   Numb were the Beadsman's fingers, while he told
His rosary, and while his frosted breath,
Like pious incense from a censer old,
Seemed taking flight for heaven, without a death,
Past the sweet Virgin's picture, while his prayer he saith.

II

10   His prayer he saith, this patient, holy man;
Then takes his lamp, and riseth from his knees,
And back returneth, meagre, barefoot, wan,
Along the chapel aisle by slow degrees:
The sculptured dead, on each side, seem to freeze,
15   Emprisoned in black, purgatorial rails;
Knights, ladies, praying in dumb orat'ries,
He passeth by; and his weak spirit fails
To think how they may ache in icy hoods and mails.

III

Northward he turneth through a little door,
20   And scarce three steps, ere Music's golden tongue
Flattered to tears this agèd man and poor;
But no – already had his deathbell rung:
The joys of all his life were said and sung:
His was harsh penance on St Agnes' Eve.
25   Another way he went, and soon among
Rough ashes sat he for his soul's reprieve,
And all night kept awake, for sinners' sake to grieve.

IV

That ancient Beadsman heard the prelude soft;
And so it chanced, for many a door was wide,
30 From hurry to and fro. Soon, up aloft,
The silver, snarling trumpets 'gan to chide:
The level chambers, ready with their pride,
Were glowing to receive a thousand guests:
The carvèd angels, ever eager-eyed,
35 Stared, where upon their heads the cornice rests,
With hair blown back, and wings put cross-wise on their
            breasts.

V

At length burst in the argent revelry,
With plume, tiara, and all rich array,
Numerous as shadows haunting faerily
40 The brain, new-stuffed, in youth, with triumphs gay
Of old romance. These let us wish away,
And turn, sole-thoughted, to one Lady there,
Whose heart had brooded, all that wintry day,
On love, and winged St Agnes' saintly care,
45 As she had heard old dames full many times declare.

VI

They told her how, upon St Agnes' Eve,
Young virgins might have visions of delight,
And soft adorings from their loves receive
Upon the honeyed middle of the night,
50 If ceremonies due they did aright;
As, supperless to bed they must retire,
And couch supine their beauties, lily white;
Nor look behind, nor sideways, but require
Of Heaven with upward eyes for all that they desire.

77

VII

55   Full of this whim was thoughtful Madeline:
The music, yearning like a God in pain,
She scarcely heard: her maiden eyes divine,
Fixed on the floor, saw many a sweeping train
Pass by – she heeded not at all: in vain
60   Came many a tip-toe, amorous cavalier,
And back retired – not cooled by high disdain,
But she saw not: her heart was otherwhere.
She sighed for Agnes' dreams, the sweetest of the year.

VIII

She danced along with vague, regardless eyes,
65   Anxious her lips, her breathing quick and short:
The hallowed hour was near at hand: she sighs
Amid the timbrels, and the thronged resort
Of whisperers in anger, or in sport;
'Mid looks of love, defiance, hate, and scorn,
70   Hoodwinked with faery fancy – all amort,
Save to St Agnes and her lambs unshorn,
And all the bliss to be before to-morrow morn.

IX

So, purposing each moment to retire,
She lingered still. Meantime, across the moors,
75   Had come young Porphyro, with heart on fire
For Madeline. Beside the portal doors,
Buttressed from moonlight, stands he, and implores
All saints to give him sight of Madeline
But for one moment in the tedious hours,
80   That he might gaze and worship all unseen;
Perchance speak, kneel, touch, kiss – in sooth such
things have been.

X

He ventures in – let not buzzed whisper tell,
All eyes be muffled, or a hundred swords
Will storm his heart, Love's fev'rous citadel:
85 For him, those chambers held barbarian hordes,
Hyena foemen, and hot-blooded lords,
Whose very dogs would execrations howl
Against his lineage: not one breast affords
Him any mercy, in that mansion foul,
90 Save one old beldame, weak in body and in soul.

XI

Ah, happy chance! the agèd creature came,
Shuffling along with ivory-headed wand,
To where he stood, hid from the torch's flame,
Behind a broad hall-pillar, far beyond
95 The sound of merriment and chorus bland:
He startled her; but soon she knew his face,
And grasped his fingers in her palsied hand,
Saying, 'Mercy, Porphyro! hie thee from this place:
They are all here to-night, the whole blood-thirsty race!

XII

100 'Get hence! get hence! there's dwarfish Hildebrand –
He had a fever late, and in the fit
He cursèd thee and thine, both house and land:
Then there's that old Lord Maurice, not a whit
More tame for his grey hairs – Alas me! flit!
105 Flit like a ghost away.' 'Ah, gossip dear,
We're safe enough; here in this arm-chair sit,
And tell me how–' 'Good Saints! not here, not here;
Follow me, child, or else these stones will be thy bier.'

XIII

He followed through a lowly archèd way,
110   Brushing the cobwebs with his lofty plume,
And as she muttered 'Well-a – well-a-day!'
He found him in a little moonlight room,
Pale, latticed, chill, and silent as a tomb.
'Now tell me where is Madeline,' said he,
115   'O tell me, Angela, by the holy loom
Which none but secret sisterhood may see,
When they St Agnes' wool are weaving piously.'

XIV

'St Agnes? Ah! it is St Agnes' Eve –
Yet men will murder upon holy days:
120   Thou must hold water in a witch's sieve,
And be liege-lord of all the Elves and Fays,
To venture so: it fills me with amaze
To see thee, Porphyro! – St Agnes' Eve!
God's help! my lady fair the conjuror plays
125   This very night. Good angels her deceive!
But let me laugh awhile, I've mickle time to grieve.'

XV

Feebly she laugheth in the languid moon,
While Porphyro upon her face doth look,
Like puzzled urchin on an agèd crone
130   Who keepeth closed a wondrous riddle-book,
As spectacled she sits in chimney nook.
But soon his eyes grew brilliant, when she told
His lady's purpose; and he scarce could brook
Tears, at the thoughts of those enchantments cold,
135 And Madeline asleep in lap of legends old.

XVI

Sudden a thought came like a full-blown rose,
Flushing his brow, and in his painèd heart
Made purple riot; then doth he propose
A stratagem, that makes the beldame start:
140 'A cruel man, and impious thou art:
Sweet lady, let her pray, and sleep, and dream
Alone with her good angels far apart
From wicked men like thee. Go, go! – I deem
Thou canst not surely be the same that thou didst seem.'

XVII

145 'I will not harm her, by all saints I swear,'
Quoth Porphyro: 'O may I ne'er find grace
When my weak voice shall whisper its last prayer,
If one of her soft ringlets I displace,
Or look with ruffian passion in her face:
150 Good Angela, believe me by these tears,
Or I will, even in a moment's space,
Awake, with horrid shout, my foeman's ears,
And beard them, though they be more fanged than
wolves and bears.'

XVIII

'Ah, why wilt thou affright a feeble soul?
155 A poor, weak, palsy-stricken, churchyard thing,
Whose passing-bell may ere the midnight toll;
Whose prayers for thee, each morn and evening,
Were never missed.' – Thus plaining, doth she bring
A gentler speech from burning Porphyro,
160 So woeful, and of such deep sorrowing,
That Angela gives promise she will do
Whatever he shall wish, betide her weal or woe.

XIX

Which was, to lead him, in close secrecy,
Even to Madeline's chamber, and there hide
165   Him in a closet, of such privacy
That he might see her beauty unespied,
And win perhaps that night a peerless bride,
While legioned faeries paced the coverlet,
And pale enchantment held her sleepy-eyed.
170   Never on such a night have lovers met,
Since Merlin paid his Demon all the monstrous debt.

XX

'It shall be as thou wishest,' said the Dame:
'All cates and dainties shall be storèd there
Quickly on this feast-night; by the tambour frame
175   Her own lute thou wilt see. No time to spare,
For I am slow and feeble, and scarce dare
On such a catering trust my dizzy head.
Wait here, my child, with patience; kneel in prayer
The while. Ah! thou must needs the lady wed,
180   Or may I never leave my grave among the dead.'

XXI

So saying, she hobbled off with busy fear.
The lover's endless minutes slowly passed;
The dame returned, and whispered in his ear
To follow her; with agèd eyes aghast
185   From fright of dim espial. Safe at last,
Through many a dusky gallery, they gain
The maiden's chamber, silken, hushed, and chaste;
Where Porphyro took covert, pleased amain.
His poor guide hurried back with agues in her brain.

XXII

190   Her faltering hand upon the balustrade,
    Old Angela was feeling for the stair,
    When Madeline, St Agnes' charmèd maid,
    Rose, like a missioned spirit, unaware:
    With silver taper's light, and pious care,
195   She turned, and down the agèd gossip led
    To a safe level matting. Now prepare,
    Young Porphyro, for gazing on that bed –
She comes, she comes again, like ring-dove frayed
        and fled.

XXIII

    Out went the taper as she hurried in;
200   Its little smoke, in pallid moonshine, died:
    She closed the door, she panted, all akin
    To spirits of the air, and visions wide –
    No uttered syllable, or, woe betide!
    But to her heart, her heart was voluble,
205   Paining with eloquence her balmy side;
    As though a tongueless nightingale should swell
Her throat in vain, and die, heart-stiflèd, in her dell.

XXIV

    A casement high and triple-arched there was,
    All garlanded with carven imag'ries
210   Of fruits, and flowers, and bunches of knot-grass,
    And diamonded with panes of quaint device,
    Innumerable of stains and splendid dyes,
    As are the tiger-moth's deep-damasked wings;
    And in the midst, 'mong thousand heraldries,
215   And twilight saints, and dim emblazonings,
A shielded scutcheon blushed with blood of queens
        and kings.

XXV

Full on this casement shone the wintry moon,
And threw warm gules on Madeline's fair breast,
As down she knelt for heaven's grace and boon;
220 Rose-bloom fell on her hands, together pressed,
And on her silver cross soft amethyst,
And on her hair a glory, like a saint:
She seemed a splendid angel, newly dressed,
Save wings, for Heaven – Porphyro grew faint;
225 She knelt, so pure a thing, so free from mortal taint.

XXVI

Anon his heart revives; her vespers done,
Of all its wreathèd pearls her hair she frees;
Unclasps her warmèd jewels one by one;
Loosens her fragrant bodice; by degrees
230 Her rich attire creeps rustling to her knees:
Half-hidden, like a mermaid in sea-weed,
Pensive awhile she dreams awake, and sees,
In fancy, fair St Agnes in her bed,
But dares not look behind, or all the charm is fled.

XXVII

235 Soon, trembling in her soft and chilly nest,
In sort of wakeful swoon, perplexed she lay,
Until the poppied warmth of sleep oppressed
Her soothèd limbs, and soul fatigued away –
Flown, like a thought, until the morrow-day;
240 Blissfully havened both from joy and pain;
Clasped like a missal where swart Paynims pray;
Blinded alike from sunshine and from rain,
As though a rose should shut, and be a bud again.

XXVIII

Stolen to this paradise, and so entranced,
245   Porphyry gazed upon her empty dress,
And listened to her breathing, if it chanced
To wake into a slumbrous tenderness;
Which when he heard, that minute did he bless,
And breathed himself: then from the closet crept,
250   Noiseless as fear in a wide wilderness,
And over the hushed carpet, silent, stepped,
And 'tween the curtains peeped, where, lo! – how fast
    she slept.

XXIX

Then by the bed-side, where the faded moon
Made a dim, silver twilight, soft he set
255   A table, and, half anguished, threw thereon
A cloth of woven crimson, gold, and jet –
O for some drowsy Morphean amulet!
The boisterous, midnight, festive clarion,
The kettle-drum, and far-heard clarinet,
260   Affray his ears, though but in dying tone;
The hall door shuts again, and all the noise is gone.

XXX

And still she slept an azure-lidded sleep,
In blanchèd linen, smooth, and lavendered,
While he from forth the closet brought a heap
265   Of candied apple, quince, and plum, and gourd,
With jellies soother than the creamy curd,
And lucent syrups, tinct with cinnamon;
Manna and dates, in argosy transferred
From Fez; and spicèd dainties, every one,
270 From silken Samarkand to cedared Lebanon.

XXXI
These delicates he heaped with glowing hand
On golden dishes and in baskets bright
Of wreathèd silver; sumptuous they stand
In the retired quiet of the night,
275   Filling the chilly room with perfume light.
'And now, my love, my seraph fair, awake!
Thou art my heaven, and I thine eremite:
Open thine eyes, for meek St Agnes' sake,
Or I shall drowse beside thee, so my soul doth ache.'

XXXII
280   Thus whispering, his warm, unnervèd arm
Sank in her pillow. Shaded was her dream
By the dusk curtains – 'twas a midnight charm
Impossible to melt as iced stream:
The lustrous salvers in the moonlight gleam;
285   Broad golden fringe upon the carpet lies.
It seemed he never, never could redeem
From such a steadfast spell his lady's eyes;
So mused awhile, entoiled in woofèd fantasies.

XXXIII
Awakening up, he took her hollow lute,
290   Tumultuous, and, in chords that tenderest be,
He played an ancient ditty, long since mute,
In Provence called, 'La belle dame sans mercy':
Close to her ear touching the melody –
Wherewith disturbed, she uttered a soft moan:
295   He ceased – she panted quick – and suddenly
Her blue affrayèd eyes wide open shone.
Upon his knees he sank, pale as smooth-sculptured
        stone.

XXXIV

    Her eyes were open, but she still beheld,
    Now wide awake, the vision of her sleep –
300   There was a painful change, that nigh expelled
    The blisses of her dream so pure and deep.
    At which fair Madeline began to weep,
    And moan forth witless words with many a sigh,
    While still her gaze on Porphyro would keep;
305   Who knelt, with joinèd hands and piteous eye,
Fearing to move or speak, she looked so dreamingly.

XXXV

    'Ah, Porphyro!' said she, 'but even now
    Thy voice was at sweet tremble in mine ear,
    Made tuneable with every sweetest vow,
310   And those sad eyes were spiritual and clear:
    How changed thou art! How pallid, chill, and drear!
    Give me that voice again, my Porphyro,
    Those looks immortal, those complainings dear!
    O leave me not in this eternal woe,
315 For if thou diest, my Love, I know not where to go.'

XXXVI

    Beyond a mortal man impassioned far
    At these voluptuous accents, he arose,
    Ethereal, flushed, and like a throbbing star
    Seen mid the sapphire heaven's deep repose;
320 Into her dream he melted, as the rose
    Blendeth its odour with the violet –
    Solution sweet. Meantime the frost-wind blows
    Like Love's alarum pattering the sharp sleet
Against the window-panes; St Agnes' moon hath set.

XXXVII

325 'Tis dark: quick pattereth the flaw-blown sleet.
'This is no dream, my bride, my Madeline!'
'Tis dark: the icèd gusts still rave and beat.
'No dream, alas! alas! and woe is mine!
Porphyro will leave me here to fade and pine. –
330 Cruel! what traitor could thee hither bring?
I curse not, for my heart is lost in thine,
Though thou forsakest a deceivèd thing –
A dove forlorn and lost with sick unprunèd wing.'

XXXVIII

'My Madeline! sweet dreamer! lovely bride!
335 Say, may I be for aye thy vassal blessed?
Thy beauty's shield, heart-shaped and vermeil dyed?
Ah, silver shrine, here will I take my rest
After so many hours of toil and quest,
A famished pilgrim – saved by miracle.
340 Though I have found, I will not rob thy nest
Saving of thy sweet self; if thou think'st well
To trust, fair Madeline, to no rude infidel.

XXXIX

'Hark! 'tis an elfin-storm from faery land,
Of haggard seeming, but a boon indeed:
345 Arise – arise! the morning is at hand.
The bloated wassaillers will never heed –
Let us away, my love, with happy speed –
There are no ears to hear, or eyes to see,
Drowned all in Rhenish and the sleepy mead;
350 Awake! arise! my love, and fearless be,
For o'er the southern moors I have a home for thee.'

XL

    She hurried at his words, beset with fears,
    For there were sleeping dragons all around,
    At glaring watch, perhaps, with ready spears –
355   Down the wide stairs a darkling way they found.
    In all the house was heard no human sound.
    A chain-drooped lamp was flickering by each door;
    The arras, rich with horseman, hawk, and hound,
    Fluttered in the besieging wind's uproar;
360 And the long carpets rose along the gusty floor.

XLI

    They glide, like phantoms, into the wide hall;
    Like phantoms, to the iron porch, they glide;
    Where lay the Porter, in uneasy sprawl,
    With a huge empty flaggon by his side:
365   The wakeful bloodhound rose, and shook his hide,
    But his sagacious eye an inmate owns.
    By one, and one, the bolts full easy slide –
    The chains lie silent on the footworn stones –
  The key turns, and the door upon its hinges groans.

XLII

370   And they are gone – ay, ages long ago
    These lovers fled away into the storm.
    That night the Baron dreamt of many a woe,
    And all his warrior-guests, with shade and form
    Of witch, and demon, and large coffin-worm,
375   Were long be-nightmared. Angela the old
    Died palsy-twitched, with meagre face deform;
    The Beadsman, after thousand aves told,
  For aye unsought for slept among his ashes cold.

The Eve of St Mark

Upon a Sabbath-day it fell;
Twice holy was the Sabbath bell,
That called the folk to evening prayer;
The city streets were clean and fair
5 From wholesome drench of April rains;
And, on the western window panes,
The chilly sunset faintly told
Of unmatured green valleys cold,
Of the green thorny bloomless hedge,
10 Of rivers new with spring-tide sedge,
Of primroses by sheltered rills,
And daisies on the aguish hills.
Twice holy was the Sabbath bell:
The silent streets were crowded well
15 With staid and pious companies,
Warm from their fireside orat'ries;
And moving, with demurest air,
To even-song, and vesper prayer.
Each archèd porch, and entry low,
20 Was filled with patient folk and slow,
With whispers hush, and shuffling feet,
While played the organs loud and sweet.

The bells had ceased, the prayers begun,
And Bertha had not yet half done
25 A curious volume, patched and torn,
That all day long, from earliest morn,
Had taken captive her two eyes,
Among its golden broideries;
Perplexed her with a thousand things –
30 The stars of Heaven, and angels' wings,
Martyrs in a fiery blaze,

Azure saints 'mid silver rays,
Aaron's breastplate, and the seven
Candlesticks John saw in Heaven,
35 The wingèd Lion of Saint Mark,
And the Covenantal Ark,
With its many mysteries,
Cherubim and golden mice.

Bertha was a maiden fair,
40 Dwelling in the old Minster Square;
From her fireside she could see,
Sidelong, its rich antiquity,
Far as the Bishop's garden-wall,
Where sycamores and elm-trees tall,
45 Full-leaved, the forest had outstripped,
By no sharp north-wind ever nipped,
So sheltered by the mighty pile.
Bertha arose, and read awhile,
With forehead 'gainst the window-pane.
50 Again she tried, and then again,
Until the dusk eve left her dark
Upon the legend of St Mark.
From pleated lawn-frill, fine and thin,
She lifted up her soft warm chin,
55 With aching neck and swimming eyes,
And dazed with saintly imageries.

All was gloom, and silent all,
Save now and then the still foot-fall
Of one returning townwards late,
60 Past the echoing Minster gate.

The clamorous daws, that all the day
Above tree-tops and towers play,

Pair by pair had gone to rest,
Each in its ancient belfry-nest,
65   Where asleep they fall betimes,
To music of the drowsy chimes.

All was silent, all was gloom,
Abroad and in the homely room:
Down she sat, poor cheated soul!
70   And struck a lamp from the dismal coal,
Leaned forward, with bright drooping hair,
And slant book full against the glare.
Her shadow, in uneasy guise,
Hovered about, a giant size,
75   On ceiling beam and old oak chair,
The parrot's cage, and panel square;
And the warm angled winter screen,
On which were many monsters seen,
Called doves of Siam, Lima mice,
80   And legless birds of Paradise,
Macaw, and tender Av'davat,
And silken-furred Angora cat.
Untired she read, her shadow still
Glowered about, as it would fill
85   The room with wildest forms and shades,
As though some ghostly Queen of Spades
Had come to mock behind her back,
And dance, and ruffle her garments black.
Untired she read the legend page,
90   Of holy Mark, from youth to age,
On land, on sea, in pagan chains,
Rejoicing for his many pains.
Sometimes the learned eremite,
With golden star, or dagger bright,
95   Referred to pious poesies

Written in smallest crow-quill size
Beneath the text; and thus the rhyme
Was parcelled out from time to time:
'– Als writith he of swevenis
100   Men han beforne they wake in bliss,
Whanne that hir friendès thinke hem bound
In crimpede shroude farre under grounde;
And how a litling child mote be
A saint er its nativitie,
105   Gif that the modre (God her blesse!)
Kepen in solitarinesse,
And kissen devoute the holy croce.
Of Goddis love, and Sathan's force,
He writith; and thinges many mo:
110   Of swichè thinges I may not show.
Bot I must tellen verilie
Somdel of Saintè Cicilie,
And chieflie what he auctorith
Of Saintè Markis life and death.'

115   At length her constant eyelids come
Upon the fervent martyrdom;
Then lastly to his holy shrine,
Exalt amid the tapers' shine
At Venice...

Bright Star

Bright star! would I were steadfast as thou art –
   Not in lone splendour hung aloft the night
And watching, with eternal lids apart,
   Like nature's patient, sleepless Eremite,
5   The moving waters at their priestlike task

Of pure ablution round earth's human shores,
Or gazing on the new soft-fallen mask
    Of snow upon the mountains and the moors –
No – yet still steadfast, still unchangeable,
10   Pillowed upon my fair love's ripening breast,
To feel for ever its soft swell and fall,
    Awake for ever in a sweet unrest,
Still, still to hear her tender-taken breath,
    And so live ever – or else swoon to death.

On a Dream

As Hermes once took to his feathers light,
    When lullèd Argus, baffled, swooned and slept,
So on a Delphic reed, my idle spright
    So played, so charmed, so conquered, so bereft
5   The dragon-world of all its hundred eyes;
    And, seeing it asleep, so fled away –
Not to pure Ida with its snow-cold skies,
    Nor unto Tempe, where Jove grieved that day;
But to that second circle of sad hell,
10   Where in the gust, the whirlwind, and the flaw
Of rain and hail-stones, lovers need not tell
    Their sorrows. Pale were the sweet lips I saw,
Pale were the lips I kissed, and fair the form
    I floated with, about that melancholy storm.

La Belle Dame sans Merci

I
O what can ail thee, knight-at-arms,
   Alone and palely loitering?
The sedge has withered from the lake,
   And no birds sing.

II
5 O what can ail thee, knight-at-arms,
   So haggard and so woe-begone?
The squirrel's granary is full,
   And the harvest's done.

III
I see a lily on thy brow,
10   With anguish moist and fever-dew,
And on thy cheeks a fading rose
   Fast withereth too.

IV
I met a lady in the meads,
   Full beautiful – a faery's child,
15 Her hair was long, her foot was light,
   And her eyes were wild.

V
I made a garland for her head,
   And bracelets too, and fragrant zone;
She looked at me as she did love,
20   And made sweet moan.

VI

I set her on my pacing steed,
    And nothing else saw all day long,
For sidelong would she bend, and sing
    A faery's song.

VII

25 She found me roots of relish sweet,
    And honey wild, and manna-dew,
And sure in language strange she said –
    'I love thee true'.

VIII

She took me to her elfin grot,
30   And there she wept and sighed full sore,
And there I shut her wild wild eyes
    With kisses four.

IX

And there she lullèd me asleep
    And there I dreamed – Ah! woe betide! –
35 The latest dream I ever dreamt
    On the cold hill side.

X

I saw pale kings and princes too,
    Pale warriors, death-pale were they all;
They cried – 'La Belle Dame sans Merci
40   Thee hath in thrall!'

XI

I saw their starved lips in the gloam,
    With horrid warning gapèd wide,
And I awoke and found me here,
    On the cold hill's side.

XII

45 And this is why I sojourn here
 Alone and palely loitering,
Though the sedge is withered from the lake,
 And no birds sing.

Ode to Psyche

O Goddess! hear these tuneless numbers, wrung
 By sweet enforcement and remembrance dear,
And pardon that thy secrets should be sung
 Even into thine own soft-conchèd ear:
5 Surely I dreamt to-day, or did I see
 The wingèd Psyche with awakened eyes?
I wandered in a forest thoughtlessly,
 And, on the sudden, fainting with surprise,
Saw two fair creatures, couchèd side by side
10 In deepest grass, beneath the whispering roof
 Of leaves and tremblèd blossoms, where there ran
  A brooklet, scarce espied:
'Mid hushed, cool-rooted flowers, fragrant-eyed,
 Blue, silver-white, and budded Tyrian,
15 They lay calm-breathing on the bedded grass;
 Their arms embraced, and their pinions too:
 Their lips touched not, but had not bade adieu,
As if disjoinèd by soft-handed slumber,
And ready still past kisses to outnumber
20 At tender eye-dawn of aurorean love:
  The wingèd boy I knew;
 But who wast thou, O happy, happy dove?
  His Psyche true!

O latest born and loveliest vision far
25   Of all Olympus' faded hierarchy!
Fairer than Phoebe's sapphire-regioned star,
    Or Vesper, amorous glow-worm of the sky;
Fairer than these, though temple thou hast none,
      Nor altar heaped with flowers;
30 Nor virgin-choir to make delicious moan
      Upon the midnight hours;
No voice, no lute, no pipe, no incense sweet
    From chain-swung censer teeming;
No shrine, no grove, no oracle, no heat
35   Of pale-mouthed prophet dreaming.

O brightest! though too late for antique vows,
    Too, too late for the fond believing lyre,
When holy were the haunted forest boughs,
    Holy the air, the water, and the fire;
40 Yet even in these days so far retired
    From happy pieties, thy lucent fans,
    Fluttering among the faint Olympians,
I see, and sing, by my own eyes inspired.
So let me be thy choir, and make a moan
45   Upon the midnight hours;
Thy voice, thy lute, thy pipe, thy incense sweet
    From swingèd censer teeming –
Thy shrine, thy grove, thy oracle, thy heat
    Of pale-mouthed prophet dreaming.

50 Yes, I will be thy priest, and build a fane
    In some untrodden region of my mind,
Where branchèd thoughts, new grown with
    pleasant pain,
    Instead of pines shall murmur in the wind:
Far, far around shall those dark-clustered trees

55   Fledge the wild-ridgèd mountains steep by steep;
    And there by zephyrs, streams, and birds, and bees,
      The moss-lain Dryads shall be lulled to sleep;
    And in the midst of this wide quietness
      A rosy sanctuary will I dress
60 With the wreathed trellis of a working brain,
      With buds, and bells, and stars without a name,
    With all the gardener Fancy e'er could feign,
      Who breeding flowers, will never breed the same:
    And there shall be for thee all soft delight
65   That shadowy thought can win,
    A bright torch, and a casement ope at night,
      To let the warm Love in!

Ode to a Nightingale

I
My heart aches, and a drowsy numbness pains
    My sense, as though of hemlock I had drunk,
Or emptied some dull opiate to the drains
    One minute past, and Lethe-wards had sunk:
5 'Tis not through envy of thy happy lot,
    But being too happy in thine happiness –
      That thou, light-wingèd Dryad of the trees,
      In some melodious plot
    Of beechen green, and shadows numberless,
10   Singest of summer in full-throated ease.

II
O, for a draught of vintage! that hath been
    Cooled a long age in the deep-delvèd earth,
Tasting of Flora and the country green,
    Dance, and Provençal song, and sunburnt mirth!

15   O for a beaker full of the warm South,
     Full of the true, the blushful Hippocrene,
       With beaded bubbles winking at the brim,
        And purple-stainèd mouth,
     That I might drink, and leave the world unseen,
20   And with thee fade away into the forest dim –

III
Fade far away, dissolve, and quite forget
     What thou among the leaves hast never known,
The weariness, the fever, and the fret
     Here, where men sit and hear each other groan;
25 Where palsy shakes a few, sad, last grey hairs,
     Where youth grows pale, and spectre-thin, and dies;
       Where but to think is to be full of sorrow
        And leaden-eyed despairs;
     Where Beauty cannot keep her lustrous eyes,
30   Or new Love pine at them beyond to-morrow.

IV
Away! away! for I will fly to thee,
     Not charioted by Bacchus and his pards,
But on the viewless wings of Poesy,
     Though the dull brain perplexes and retards.
35 Already with thee! tender is the night,
     And haply the Queen-Moon is on her throne,
       Clustered around by all her starry Fays;
        But here there is no light,
     Save what from heaven is with the breezes blown
40   Through verdurous glooms and winding
          mossy ways.

V

I cannot see what flowers are at my feet,
 Nor what soft incense hangs upon the boughs,
But, in embalmèd darkness, guess each sweet
 Wherewith the seasonable month endows
45 The grass, the thicket, and the fruit-tree wild –
  White hawthorn, and the pastoral eglantine;
   Fast fading violets covered up in leaves;
    And mid-May's eldest child,
  The coming musk-rose, full of dewy wine,
50   The murmurous haunt of flies on summer eves.

VI

Darkling I listen; and, for many a time
 I have been half in love with easeful Death,
Called him soft names in many a musèd rhyme,
 To take into the air my quiet breath;
55 Now more than ever seems it rich to die,
  To cease upon the midnight with no pain,
   While thou art pouring forth thy soul abroad
    In such an ecstasy!
  Still wouldst thou sing, and I have ears in vain –
60   To thy high requiem become a sod.

VII

Thou wast not born for death, immortal Bird!
 No hungry generations tread thee down;
The voice I hear this passing night was heard
 In ancient days by emperor and clown:
65 Perhaps the self-same song that found a path
  Through the sad heart of Ruth, when, sick for home,
   She stood in tears amid the alien corn;
    The same that oft-times hath
  Charmed magic casements, opening on the foam
70   Of perilous seas, in faery lands forlorn.

VIII
Forlorn! the very word is like a bell
  To toll me back from thee to my sole self!
Adieu! the fancy cannot cheat so well
  As she is famed to do, deceiving elf.
75 Adieu! adieu! thy plaintive anthem fades
    Past the near meadows, over the still stream,
      Up the hill-side; and now 'tis buried deep
      In the next valley-glades:
    Was it a vision, or a waking dream?
80   Fled is that music – Do I wake or sleep?

Ode on a Grecian Urn

I
Thou still unravished bride of quietness,
  Thou foster-child of silence and slow time,
Sylvan historian, who canst thus express
  A flowery tale more sweetly than our rhyme:
5 What leaf-fringed legend haunts about thy shape
    Of deities or mortals, or of both,
      In Tempe or the dales of Arcady?
    What men or gods are these? What maidens loth?
What mad pursuit? What struggle to escape?
10   What pipes and timbrels? What wild ecstasy?

II
Heard melodies are sweet, but those unheard
  Are sweeter; therefore, ye soft pipes, play on;
Not to the sensual ear, but, more endeared,
  Pipe to the spirit ditties of no tone:
15 Fair youth, beneath the trees, thou canst not leave
    Thy song, nor ever can those trees be bare;

Bold Lover, never, never canst thou kiss,
Though winning near the goal – yet, do not grieve;
She cannot fade, though thou hast not thy bliss,
20   For ever wilt thou love, and she be fair!

III
Ah, happy, happy boughs! that cannot shed
Your leaves, nor ever bid the Spring adieu;
And, happy melodist, unwearièd,
For ever piping songs for ever new;
25 More happy love! more happy, happy love!
For ever warm and still to be enjoyed,
For ever panting, and for ever young –
All breathing human passion far above,
That leaves a heart high-sorrowful and cloyed,
30   A burning forehead, and a parching tongue.

IV
Who are these coming to the sacrifice?
To what green altar, O mysterious priest,
Lead'st thou that heifer lowing at the skies,
And all her silken flanks with garlands dressed?
35 What little town by river or sea shore,
Or mountain-built with peaceful citadel,
Is emptied of this folk, this pious morn?
And, little town, thy streets for evermore
Will silent be; and not a soul to tell
40   Why thou art desolate, can e'er return.

V
O Attic shape! Fair attitude! with brede
Of marble men and maidens overwrought,
With forest branches and the trodden weed;
Thou, silent form, dost tease us out of thought

45 As doth eternity: Cold Pastoral!
  When old age shall this generation waste,
   Thou shalt remain, in midst of other woe
  Than ours, a friend to man, to whom thou say'st,
   'Beauty is truth, truth beauty, – that is all
50   Ye know on earth, and all ye need to know.'

Ode on Melancholy

I

No, no, go not to Lethe, neither twist
  Wolf's-bane, tight-rooted, for its poisonous wine:
Nor suffer thy pale forehead to be kissed
  By nightshade, ruby grape of Proserpine;
5 Make not your rosary of yew-berries,
   Nor let the beetle, nor the death-moth be
    Your mournful Psyche, nor the downy owl
A partner in your sorrow's mysteries;
   For shade to shade will come too drowsily,
10   And drown the wakeful anguish of the soul.

II

But when the melancholy fit shall fall
  Sudden from heaven like a weeping cloud,
That fosters the droop-headed flowers all,
  And hides the green hill in an April shroud;
15 Then glut thy sorrow on a morning rose,
   Or on the rainbow of the salt sand-wave,
    Or on the wealth of globèd peonies;
Or if thy mistress some rich anger shows,
   Emprison her soft hand, and let her rave,
20   And feed deep, deep upon her peerless eyes.

III
She dwells with Beauty – Beauty that must die;
    And Joy, whose hand is ever at his lips
Bidding adieu; and aching Pleasure nigh,
    Turning to poison while the bee-mouth sips:
25 Ay, in the very temple of Delight
        Veiled Melancholy has her sovran shrine,
            Though seen of none save him whose strenuous
                tongue
        Can burst Joy's grape against his palate fine;
His soul shall taste the sadness of her might,
30   And be among her cloudy trophies hung.

Ode on Indolence
'*They toil not, neither do they spin.*'

I
One morn before me were three figures seen,
    With bowèd necks, and joinèd hands, side-faced;
And one behind the other stepped serene,
    In placid sandals, and in white robes graced;
5 They passed, like figures on a marble urn,
        When shifted round to see the other side;
            They came again; as when the urn once more
        Is shifted round, the first seen shades return;
            And they were strange to me, as may betide
10   With vases, to one deep in Phidian lore.

II
How is it, Shadows! that I knew ye not?
    How came ye muffled in so hush a masque?
Was it a silent deep-disguisèd plot
    To steal away, and leave without a task

15 My idle days? Ripe was the drowsy hour;
        The blissful cloud of summer-indolence
            Benumbed my eyes; my pulse grew less and less;
        Pain had no sting, and pleasure's wreath no flower:
            O, why did ye not melt, and leave my sense
20   Unhaunted quite of all but – nothingness?

        III
        A third time passed they by, and, passing, turned
            Each one the face a moment whiles to me;
        Then faded, and to follow them I burned
            And ached for wings because I knew the three;
25 The first was a fair Maid, and Love her name;
        The second was Ambition, pale of cheek,
            And ever watchful with fatiguèd eye;
        The last, whom I love more, the more of blame
            Is heaped upon her, maiden most unmeek –
30   I knew to be my demon Poesy.

        IV
        They faded, and, forsooth! I wanted wings.
            O folly! What is love? and where is it?
        And, for that poor Ambition – it springs
            From a man's little heart's short fever-fit.
35 For Poesy! – no, she has not a joy –
            At least for me – so sweet as drowsy noons,
                And evenings steeped in honeyed indolence.
        O, for an age so sheltered from annoy,
            That I may never know how change the moons,
40   Or hear the voice of busy common-sense!

V
A third time came they by – alas! wherefore?
  My sleep had been embroidered with dim dreams;
  My soul had been a lawn besprinkled o'er
    With flowers, and stirring shades, and baffled beams:
45 The morn was clouded, but no shower fell,
    Though in her lids hung the sweet tears of May;
      The open casement pressed a new-leaved vine,
    Let in the budding warmth and throstle's lay;
  O Shadows! 'twas a time to bid farewell!
50   Upon your skirts had fallen no tears of mine.

VI
So, ye three Ghosts, adieu! Ye cannot raise
  My head cool-bedded in the flowery grass;
For I would not be dieted with praise,
  A pet-lamb in a sentimental farce!
55 Fade softly from my eyes, and be once more
    In masque-like figures on the dreamy urn.
      Farewell! I yet have visions for the night,
And for the day faint visions there is store.
      Vanish, ye Phantoms! from my idle sprite,
60   Into the clouds, and never more return!

Lamia

Part I
Upon a time, before the faery broods
Drove Nymph and Satyr from the prosperous woods,
Before King Oberon's bright diadem,
Sceptre, and mantle, clasped with dewy gem,
5 Frighted away the Dryads and the Fauns
From rushes green, and brakes, and cowslipped lawns,

The ever-smitten Hermes empty left
His golden throne, bent warm on amorous theft:
From high Olympus had he stolen light,
10 On this side of Jove's clouds, to escape the sight
Of his great summoner, and made retreat
Into a forest on the shores of Crete.
For somewhere in that sacred island dwelt
A nymph, to whom all hoofèd Satyrs knelt,
15 At whose white feet the languid Tritons poured
Pearls, while on land they withered and adored.
Fast by the springs where she to bathe was wont,
And in those meads where sometime she might haunt,
Were strewn rich gifts, unknown to any Muse,
20 Though Fancy's casket were unlocked to choose.
Ah, what a world of love was at her feet!
So Hermes thought, and a celestial heat
Burnt from his wingèd heels to either ear,
That from a whiteness, as the lily clear,
25 Blushed into roses 'mid his golden hair,
Fallen in jealous curls about his shoulders bare.

From vale to vale, from wood to wood, he flew,
Breathing upon the flowers his passion new,
And wound with many a river to its head,
30 To find where this sweet nymph prepared her secret bed.
In vain; the sweet nymph might nowhere be found,
And so he rested, on the lonely ground,
Pensive, and full of painful jealousies
Of the Wood-Gods, and even the very trees.
35 There as he stood, he heard a mournful voice,
Such as, once heard, in gentle heart destroys
All pain but pity; thus the lone voice spake:
'When from this wreathèd tomb shall I awake!
When move in a sweet body fit for life,

40 And love, and pleasure, and the ruddy strife
    Of hearts and lips! Ah, miserable me!'
    The God, dove-footed, glided silently
    Round bush and tree, soft-brushing, in his speed,
    The taller grasses and full-flowering weed,
45 Until he found a palpitating snake,
    Bright, and cirque-couchant in a dusky brake.

    She was a gordian shape of dazzling hue,
    Vermilion-spotted, golden, green, and blue;
    Striped like a zebra, freckled like a pard,
50 Eyed like a peacock, and all crimson barred;
    And full of silver moons, that, as she breathed,
    Dissolved, or brighter shone, or interwreathed
    Their lustres with the gloomier tapestries –
    So rainbow-sided, touched with miseries,
55 She seemed, at once, some penanced lady elf,
    Some demon's mistress, or the demon's self.
    Upon her crest she wore a wannish fire
    Sprinkled with stars, like Ariadne's tiar;
    Her head was serpent, but ah, bitter-sweet!
60 She had a woman's mouth with all its pearls complete;
    And for her eyes – what could such eyes do there
    But weep, and weep, that they were born so fair,
    As Proserpine still weeps for Sicilian air.
    Her throat was serpent, but the words she spake
65 Came, as through bubbling honey, for Love's sake,
    And thus – while Hermes on his pinions lay,
    Like a stooped falcon ere he takes his prey –

    'Fair Hermes, crowned with feathers, fluttering light,
    I had a splendid dream of thee last night:
70 I saw thee sitting, on a throne of gold,
    Among the Gods, upon Olympus old,

The only sad one; for thou didst not hear
The soft, lute-fingered Muses chanting clear,
Nor even Apollo when he sang alone,
75 Deaf to his throbbing throat's long, long melodious
          moan.
I dreamt I saw thee, robed in purple flakes,
Break amorous through the clouds, as morning breaks,
And, swiftly as a bright Phoebean dart,
Strike for the Cretan isle; and here thou art!
80 Too gentle Hermes, hast thou found the maid?'
Whereat the star of Lethe not delayed
His rosy eloquence, and thus inquired:
'Thou smooth-lipped serpent, surely high inspired!
Thou beauteous wreath, with melancholy eyes,
85 Possess whatever bliss thou canst devise,
Telling me only where my nymph is fled –
Where she doth breathe!' 'Bright planet, thou hast said,'
Returned the snake, 'but seal with oaths, fair God!'
'I swear,' said Hermes, 'by my serpent rod,
90 And by thine eyes, and by thy starry crown!'
Light flew his earnest words, among the blossoms blown.
Then thus again the brilliance feminine:
'Too frail of heart! for this lost nymph of thine,
Free as the air, invisibly, she strays
95 About these thornless wilds; her pleasant days
She tastes unseen; unseen her nimble feet
Leave traces in the grass and flowers sweet;
From weary tendrils, and bowed branches green,
She plucks the fruit unseen, she bathes unseen;
100 And by my power is her beauty veiled
To keep it unaffronted, unassailed
By the love-glances of unlovely eyes
Of Satyrs, Fauns, and bleared Silenus' sighs.
Pale grew her immortality, for woe

105 Of all these lovers, and she grievèd so
I took compassion on her, bade her steep
Her hair in weïrd syrops, that would keep
Her loveliness invisible, yet free
To wander as she loves, in liberty.
110 Thou shalt behold her, Hermes, thou alone,
If thou wilt, as thou swearest, grant my boon!'
Then, once again, the charmèd God began
An oath, and through the serpent's ears it ran
Warm, tremulous, devout, psalterian.
115 Ravished, she lifted her Circean head,
Blushed a live damask, and swift-lisping said,
'I was a woman, let me have once more
A woman's shape, and charming as before.
I love a youth of Corinth – O the bliss!
120 Give me my woman's form, and place me where he is.
Stoop, Hermes, let me breathe upon thy brow,
And thou shalt see thy sweet nymph even now.'
The God on half-shut feather sank serene,
She breathed upon his eyes, and swift was seen
125 Of both the guarded nymph near-smiling on the green.
It was no dream; or say a dream it was,
Real are the dreams of Gods, and smoothly pass
Their pleasures in a long immortal dream.
One warm, flushed moment, hovering, it might seem
130 Dashed by the wood-nymph's beauty, so he burned;
Then, lighting on the printless verdure, turned
To the swooned serpent, and with languid arm,
Delicate, put to proof the lithe Caducean charm.
So done, upon the nymph his eyes he bent
135 Full of adoring tears and blandishment,
And towards her stepped: she, like a moon in wane,
Faded before him, cowered, nor could restrain
Her fearful sobs, self-folding like a flower

That faints into itself at evening hour:
140   But the God fostering her chillèd hand,
She felt the warmth, her eyelids opened bland,
And, like new flowers at morning song of bees,
Bloomed, and gave up her honey to the lees.
Into the green-recessèd woods they flew;
145   Nor grew they pale, as mortal lovers do.

     Left to herself, the serpent now began
To change; her elfin blood in madness ran,
Her mouth foamed, and the grass, therewith besprent,
Withered at dew so sweet and virulent;
150   Her eyes in torture fixed, and anguish drear,
Hot, glazed, and wide, with lid-lashes all sear,
Flashed phosphor and sharp sparks, without one cooling
        tear.
The colours all inflamed throughout her train,
She writhed about, convulsed with scarlet pain:
155   A deep volcanian yellow took the place
Of all her milder-moonèd body's grace;
And, as the lava ravishes the mead,
Spoilt all her silver mail, and golden brede;
Made gloom of all her frecklings, streaks and bars,
160   Eclipsed her crescents, and licked up her stars.
So that, in moments few, she was undressed
Of all her sapphires, greens, and amethyst,
And rubious-argent; of all these bereft,
Nothing but pain and ugliness were left.
165   Still shone her crown; that vanished, also she
Melted and disappeared as suddenly;
And in the air, her new voice luting soft,
Cried, 'Lycius! gentle Lycius!' – Borne aloft
With the bright mists about the mountains hoar
170   These words dissolved: Crete's forests heard no more.

     Whither fled Lamia, now a lady bright,
A full-born beauty new and exquisite?
She fled into that valley they pass o'er
Who go to Corinth from Cenchreas' shore;
175 And rested at the foot of those wild hills,
The rugged founts of the Peraean rills,
And of that other ridge whose barren back
Stretched, with all its mist and cloudy rack,
South-westward to Cleone. There she stood
180 About a young bird's flutter from a wood,
Fair, on a sloping green of mossy tread,
By a clear pool, wherein she passionèd
To see herself escaped from so sore ills,
While her robes flaunted with the daffodils.

185   Ah, happy Lycius! – for she was a maid
More beautiful than ever twisted braid,
Or sighed, or blushed, or on spring-flowered lea
Spread a green kirtle to the minstrelsy:
A virgin purest lipped, yet in the lore
190 Of love deep learnèd to the red heart's core;
Not one hour old, yet of sciential brain
To unperplex bliss from its neighbour pain;
Define their pettish limits, and estrange
Their points of contact, and swift counterchange;
195 Intrigue with the specious chaos, and dispart
Its most ambiguous atoms with sure art;
As though in Cupid's college she had spent
Sweet days a lovely graduate, still unshent,
And kept his rosy terms in idle languishment.

200   Why this fair creature chose so faerily
By the wayside to linger, we shall see;
But first 'tis fit to tell how she could muse

And dream, when in the serpent prison-house,
Of all she list, strange or magnificent:
205 How, ever, where she willed, her spirit went;
Whether to faint Elysium, or where
Down through tress-lifting waves the Nereids fair
Wind into Thetis' bower by many a pearly stair;
Or where God Bacchus drains his cup divine,
210 Stretched out, at ease, beneath a glutinous pine;
Or where in Pluto's gardens palatine
Mulciber's columns gleam in far piazzian line.
And sometimes into cities she would send
Her dream, with feast and rioting to blend;
215 And once, while among mortals dreaming thus,
She saw the young Corinthian Lycius
Charioting foremost in the envious race,
Like a young Jove with calm uneager face,
And fell into a swooning love of him.
220 Now on the moth-time of that evening dim
He would return that way, as well she knew,
To Corinth from the shore; for freshly blew
The eastern soft wind, and his galley now
Grated the quaystones with her brazen prow
225 In port Cenchreas, from Egina isle
Fresh anchored; whither he had been awhile
To sacrifice to Jove, whose temple there
Waits with high marble doors for blood and incense rare.
Jove heard his vows, and bettered his desire;
230 For by some freakful chance he made retire
From his companions, and set forth to walk,
Perhaps grown wearied of their Corinth talk:
Over the solitary hills he fared,
Thoughtless at first, but ere eve's star appeared
235 His fantasy was lost, where reason fades,
In the calmed twilight of Platonic shades.

Lamia beheld him coming, near, more near –
Close to her passing, in indifference drear,
His silent sandals swept the mossy green;
240 So neighboured to him, and yet so unseen
She stood: he passed, shut up in mysteries,
His mind wrapped like his mantle, while her eyes
Followed his steps, and her neck regal white
Turned – syllabling thus, 'Ah, Lycius bright,
245 And will you leave me on the hills alone?
Lycius, look back! and be some pity shown.'
He did – not with cold wonder fearingly,
But Orpheus-like at an Eurydice –
For so delicious were the words she sung,
250 It seemed he had loved them a whole summer long.
And soon his eyes had drunk her beauty up,
Leaving no drop in the bewildering cup,
And still the cup was full – while he, afraid
Lest she should vanish ere his lip had paid
255 Due adoration, thus began to adore
(Her soft look growing coy, she saw his chain so sure):
'Leave thee alone! Look back! Ah, Goddess, see
Whether my eyes can ever turn from thee!
For pity do not this sad heart belie –
260 Even as thou vanished so shall I die.
Stay! though a Naiad of the rivers, stay!
To thy far wishes will thy streams obey.
Stay! though the greenest woods be thy domain,
Alone they can drink up the morning rain:
265 Though a descended Pleiad, will not one
Of thine harmonious sisters keep in tune
Thy spheres, and as thy silver proxy shine?
So sweetly to these ravished ears of mine
Came thy sweet greeting, that if thou shouldst fade
270 Thy memory will waste me to a shade –

For pity do not melt!' – 'If I should stay,'
Said Lamia, 'here, upon this floor of clay,
And pain my steps upon these flowers too rough,
What canst thou say or do of charm enough
275   To dull the nice remembrance of my home?
Thou canst not ask me with thee here to roam
Over these hills and vales, where no joy is –
Empty of immortality and bliss!
Thou art a scholar, Lycius, and must know
280   That finer spirits cannot breathe below
In human climes, and live. Alas! poor youth,
What taste of purer air hast thou to soothe
My essence? What serener palaces,
Where I may all my many senses please,
285   And by mysterious sleights a hundred thirsts appease?
It cannot be – Adieu!' So said, she rose
Tip-toe with white arms spread. He, sick to lose
The amorous promise of her lone complain,
Swooned, murmuring of love, and pale with pain.
290   The cruel lady, without any show
Of sorrow for her tender favourite's woe,
But rather, if her eyes could brighter be,
With brighter eyes and slow amenity,
Put her new lips to his, and gave afresh
295   The life she had so tangled in her mesh;
And as he from one trance was wakening
Into another, she began to sing,
Happy in beauty, life, and love, and every thing,
A song of love, too sweet for earthly lyres,
300   While, like held breath, the stars drew in their
             panting fires.
And then she whispered in such trembling tone,
As those who, safe together met alone
For the first time through many anguished days,

Use other speech than looks; bidding him raise
305 His drooping head, and clear his soul of doubt,
For that she was a woman, and without
Any more subtle fluid in her veins
Than throbbing blood, and that the self-same pains
Inhabited her frail-strung heart as his.
310 And next she wondered how his eyes could miss
Her face so long in Corinth, where, she said,
She dwelt but half retired, and there had led
Days happy as the gold coin could invent
Without the aid of love; yet in content
315 Till she saw him, as once she passed him by,
Where 'gainst a column he leant thoughtfully
At Venus' temple porch, 'mid baskets heaped
Of amorous herbs and flowers, newly reaped
Late on that eve, as 'twas the night before
320 The Adonian feast; whereof she saw no more,
But wept alone those days, for why should she adore?
Lycius from death awoke into amaze,
To see her still, and singing so sweet lays;
Then from amaze into delight he fell
325 To hear her whisper woman's lore so well;
And every word she spake enticed him on
To unperplexed delight and pleasure known.
Let the mad poets say whate'er they please
Of the sweets of Faeries, Peris, Goddesses,
330 There is not such a treat among them all,
Haunters of cavern, lake, and waterfall,
As a real woman, lineal indeed
From Pyrrha's pebbles or old Adam's seed.
Thus gentle Lamia judged, and judged aright,
335 That Lycius could not love in half a fright,
So threw the goddess off, and won his heart
More pleasantly by playing woman's part,

With no more awe than what her beauty gave,
That, while it smote, still guaranteed to save.
340 Lycius to all made eloquent reply,
Marrying to every word a twinborn sigh;
And last, pointing to Corinth, asked her sweet,
It 'twas too far that night for her soft feet.
The way was short, for Lamia's eagerness
345 Made, by a spell, the triple league decrease
To a few paces; not at all surmised
By blinded Lycius, so in her comprised.
They passed the city gates, he knew not how,
So noiseless, and he never thought to know.

350 As men talk in a dream, so Corinth all,
Throughout her palaces imperial,
And all her populous streets and temples lewd,
Muttered, like tempest in the distance brewed,
To the wide-spreaded night above her towers.
355 Men, women, rich and poor, in the cool hours,
Shuffled their sandals o'er the pavement white,
Companioned or alone; while many a light
Flared, here and there, from wealthy festivals,
And threw their moving shadows on the walls,
360 Or found them clustered in the corniced shade
Of some arched temple door, or dusky colonnade.

Muffling his face, of greeting friends in fear,
Her fingers he pressed hard, as one came near
With curled grey beard, sharp eyes, and smooth bald
crown,
365 Slow-stepped, and robed in philosophic gown:
Lycius shrank closer, as they met and passed,
Into his mantle, adding wings to haste,
While hurried Lamia trembled: 'Ah,' said he,

'Why do you shudder, love, so ruefully?
370 Why does your tender palm dissolve in dew?' –
'I'm wearied,' said fair Lamia: 'tell me who
Is that old man? I cannot bring to mind
His features – Lycius! wherefore did you blind
Yourself from his quick eyes?' Lycius replied,
375 ''Tis Apollonius sage, my trusty guide
And good instructor; but tonight he seems
The ghost of folly haunting my sweet dreams.'

    While yet he spake they had arrived before
A pillared porch, with lofty portal door,
380 Where hung a silver lamp, whose phosphor glow
Reflected in the slabbèd steps below,
Mild as a star in water; for so new,
And so unsullied was the marble hue,
So through the crystal polish, liquid fine,
385 Ran the dark veins, that none but feet divine
Could e'er have touched there. Sounds Aeolian
Breathed from the hinges, as the ample span
Of the wide doors disclosed a place unknown
Some time to any, but those two alone,
390 And a few Persian mutes, who at that same year
Were seen about the markets: none knew where
They could inhabit; the most curious
Were foiled, who watched to trace them to their house.
And but the flitter-wingèd verse must tell
395 For truth's sake, what woe afterwards befell,
'Twould humour many a heart to leave them thus,
Shut from the busy world, of more incredulous.

Part II
Love in a hut, with water and a crust,
Is – Love, forgive us! – cinders, ashes, dust;
Love in a palace is perhaps at last
More grievous torment than a hermit's fast.
5   That is a doubtful tale from faery land,
Hard for the non-elect to understand.
Had Lycius lived to hand his story down,
He might have given the moral a fresh frown,
Or clenched it quite: but too short was their bliss
10   To breed distrust and hate, that make the soft voice hiss.
Besides, there, nightly, with terrific glare,
Love, jealous grown of so complete a pair,
Hovered and buzzed his wings, with fearful roar,
Above the lintel of their chamber door,
15   And down the passage cast a glow upon the floor.

For all this came a ruin: side by side
They were enthronèd, in the eventide,
Upon a couch, near to a curtaining
Whose airy texture, from a golden string,
20   Floated into the room, and let appear
Unveiled the summer heaven, blue and clear,
Betwixt two marble shafts. There they reposed,
Where use had made it sweet, with eyelids closed,
Saving a tithe which love still open kept,
25   That they might see each other while they almost slept;
When from the slope side of a suburb hill,
Deafening the swallow's twitter, came a thrill
Of trumpets – Lycius started – the sounds fled,
But left a thought, a buzzing in his head.
30   For the first time, since first he harboured in
That purple-linèd palace of sweet sin,
His spirit passed beyond its golden bourne

Into the noisy world almost forsworn.
The lady, ever watchful, penetrant,
35 Saw this with pain, so arguing a want
Of something more, more than her empery
Of joys; and she began to moan and sigh
Because he mused beyond her, knowing well
That but a moment's thought is passion's passing-bell.
40 'Why do you sigh, fair creature?' whisper'd he:
'Why do you think?' returned she tenderly,
'You have deserted me – where am I now?
Not in your heart while care weighs on your brow:
No, no, you have dismissed me; and I go
45 From your breast houseless – ay, it must be so.'
He answered, bending to her open eyes,
Where he was mirrored small in paradise,
'My silver planet, both of eve and morn!
Why will you plead yourself so sad forlorn,
50 While I am striving how to fill my heart
With deeper crimson, and a double smart?
How to entangle, trammel up and snare
Your soul in mine, and labyrinth you there
Like the hid scent in an unbudded rose?
55 Ay, a sweet kiss – you see your mighty woes.
My thoughts! shall I unveil them? Listen then!
What mortal hath a prize, that other men
May be confounded and abashed withal,
But lets it sometimes pace abroad majestical,
60 And triumph, as in thee I should rejoice
Amid the hoarse alarm of Corinth's voice.
Let my foes choke, and my friends shout afar,
While through the throngèd streets your bridal car
Wheels round its dazzling spokes.' – The lady's cheek
65 Trembled; she nothing said, but, pale and meek,
Arose and knelt before him, wept a rain

Of sorrows at his words; at last with pain
Beseeching him, the while his hand she wrung,
To change his purpose. He thereat was stung,
70 Perverse, with stronger fancy to reclaim
Her wild and timid nature to his aim:
Besides, for all his love, in self-despite,
Against his better self, he took delight
Luxurious in her sorrows, soft and new.
75 His passion, cruel grown, took on a hue
Fierce and sanguineous as 'twas possible
In one whose brow had no dark veins to swell.
Fine was the mitigated fury, like
Apollo's presence when in act to strike
80 The serpent – Ha, the serpent! Certes, she
Was none. She burnt, she loved the tyranny,
And, all subdued, consented to the hour
When to the bridal he should lead his paramour.
Whispering in the midnight silence, said the youth,
85 'Sure some sweet name thou hast, though, by my
         truth,
I have not asked it, ever thinking thee
Not mortal, but of heavenly progeny,
As still I do. Hast any mortal name,
Fit appellation for this dazzling frame?
90 Or friends or kinsfolk on the citied earth,
To share our marriage feast and nuptial mirth?'
'I have no friends,' said Lamia, 'no, no one;
My presence in wide Corinth hardly known:
My parents' bones are in their dusty urns
95 Sepulchred, where no kindled incense burns,
Seeing all their luckless race are dead, save me,
And I neglect the holy rite for thee.
Even as you list invite your many guests;
But if, as now it seems, your vision rests

100 With any pleasure on me, do not bid
　　Old Apollonius – from him keep me hid.'
　　Lycius, perplexed at words so blind and blank,
　　Made close inquiry; from whose touch she shrank,
　　Feigning a sleep; and he to the dull shade
105 Of deep sleep in a moment was betrayed.

　　　It was the custom then to bring away
　　The bride from home at blushing shut of day,
　　Veiled, in a chariot, heralded along
　　By strewn flowers, torches, and a marriage song,
110 With other pageants: but this fair unknown
　　Had not a friend. So being left alone,
　　(Lycius was gone to summon all his kin)
　　And knowing surely she could never win
　　His foolish heart from its mad pompousness,
115 She set herself, high-thoughted, how to dress
　　The misery in fit magnificence.
　　She did so, but 'tis doubtful how and whence
　　Came, and who were her subtle servitors.
　　About the halls, and to and from the doors,
120 There was a noise of wings, till in short space
　　The glowing banquet-room shone with wide-archèd
　　　　grace.
　　A haunting music, sole perhaps and lone
　　Supportress of the faery-roof, made moan
　　Throughout, as fearful the whole charm might fade.
125 Fresh carvèd cedar, mimicking a glade
　　Of palm and plantain, met from either side,
　　High in the midst, in honour of the bride;
　　Two palms and then two plantains, and so on,
　　From either side their stems branched one to one
130 All down the aislèd place; and beneath all

There ran a stream of lamps straight on from wall to
    wall.
So canopied, lay an untasted feast
Teeming with odours. Lamia, regal dressed,
Silently paced about, and as she went,
135   In pale contented sort of discontent,
Missioned her viewless servants to enrich
The fretted splendour of each nook and niche.
Between the tree-stems, marbled plain at first,
Came jasper panels; then, anon, there burst
140   Forth creeping imagery of slighter trees,
And with the larger wove in small intricacies.
Approving all, she faded at self-will,
And shut the chamber up, close, hushed and still,
Complete and ready for the revels rude,
145   When dreadful guests would come to spoil her solitude.

    The day appeared, and all the gossip rout.
O senseless Lycius! Madman! wherefore flout
The silent-blessing fate, warm cloistered hours,
And show to common eyes these secret bowers?
150   The herd approached; each guest, with busy brain,
Arriving at the portal, gazed amain,
And entered marvelling – for they knew the street,
Remembered it from childhood all complete
Without a gap, yet ne'er before had seen
155   That royal porch, that high-built fair demesne.
So in they hurried all, mazed, curious and keen –
Save one, who looked thereon with eye severe,
And with calm-planted steps walked in austere.
'Twas Apollonius: something too he laughed,
160   As though some knotty problem, that had daffed
His patient thought, had now begun to thaw,
And solve and melt – 'twas just as he foresaw.

He met within the murmurous vestibule
His young disciple. ''Tis no common rule,
165 Lycius,' said he, 'for uninvited guest
To force himself upon you, and infest
With an unbidden presence the bright throng
Of younger friends; yet must I do this wrong,
And you forgive me.' Lycius blushed, and led
170 The old man through the inner doors broad-spread;
With reconciling words and courteous mien
Turning into sweet milk the sophist's spleen.

Of wealthy lustre was the banquet-room,
Filled with pervading brilliance and perfume:
175 Before each lucid panel fuming stood
A censer fed with myrrh and spicèd wood,
Each by a sacred tripod held aloft,
Whose slender feet wide-swerved upon the soft
Wool-woofèd carpets; fifty wreaths of smoke
180 From fifty censers their light voyage took
To the high roof, still mimicked as they rose
Along the mirrored walls by twin-clouds odorous.
Twelve spherèd tables, by silk seats enspherèd,
High as the level of a man's breast reared
185 On libbard's paws, upheld the heavy gold
Of cups and goblets, and the store thrice told
Of Ceres' horn, and, in huge vessels, wine
Come from the gloomy tun with merry shine.
Thus loaded with a feast the tables stood,
190 Each shrining in the midst the image of a God.

When in an antichamber every guest
Had felt the cold full sponge to pleasure pressed,
By ministering slaves, upon his hands and feet,
And fragrant oils with ceremony meet

195　Poured on his hair, they all moved to the feast
　　In white robes, and themselves in order placed
　　Around the silken couches, wondering
　　Whence all this mighty cost and blaze of wealth
　　　　could spring.

　　Soft went the music the soft air along,
200　While fluent Greek a vowelled undersong
　　Kept up among the guests, discoursing low
　　At first, for scarcely was the wine at flow;
　　But when the happy vintage touched their brains,
　　Louder they talk, and louder come the strains
205　Of powerful instruments. The gorgeous dyes,
　　The space, the splendour of the draperies,
　　The roof of awful richness, nectarous cheer,
　　Beautiful slaves, and Lamia's self, appear,
　　Now, when the wine has done its rosy deed,
210　And every soul from human trammels freed,
　　No more so strange; for merry wine, sweet wine,
　　Will make Elysian shades not too fair, too divine.

　　Soon was God Bacchus at meridian height;
　　Flushed were their cheeks, and bright eyes double
　　　　bright:
215　Garlands of every green, and every scent
　　From vales deflowered, or forest-trees branch-rent,
　　In baskets of bright osiered gold were brought
　　High as the handles heaped, to suit the thought
　　Of every guest – that each, as he did please,
220　Might fancy-fit his brows, silk-pillowed at his ease.

　　What wreath for Lamia? What for Lycius?
　　What for the sage, old Apollonius?
　　Upon her aching forehead be there hung

The leaves of willow and of adder's tongue;
225 And for the youth, quick, let us strip for him
The thyrsus, that his watching eyes may swim
Into forgetfulness; and, for the sage,
Let spear-grass and the spiteful thistle wage
War on his temples. Do not all charms fly
230 At the mere touch of cold philosophy?
There was an awful rainbow once in heaven:
We know her woof, her texture; she is given
In the dull catalogue of common things.
Philosophy will clip an Angel's wings,
235 Conquer all mysteries by rule and line,
Empty the haunted air, and gnomèd mine –
Unweave a rainbow, as it erewhile made
The tender-personed Lamia melt into a shade.

By her glad Lycius sitting, in chief place,
240 Scarce saw in all the room another face,
Till, checking his love trance, a cup he took
Full brimmed, and opposite set forth a look
'Cross the broad table, to beseech a glance
From his old teacher's wrinkled countenance,
245 And pledge him. The bald-head philosopher
Had fixed his eye, without a twinkle or stir
Full on the alarmèd beauty of the bride,
Brow-beating her fair form, and troubling her sweet
        pride.
Lycius then pressed her hand, with devout touch,
250 As pale it lay upon the rosy couch:
'Twas icy, and the cold ran through his veins;
Then sudden it grew hot, and all the pains
Of an unnatural heat shot to his heart.
'Lamia, what means this? Wherefore dost thou start?
255 Know'st thou that man?' Poor Lamia answered not.

He gazed into her eyes, and not a jot
Owned they the lovelorn piteous appeal;
More, more he gazed; his human senses reel;
Some hungry spell that loveliness absorbs;
260   There was no recognition in those orbs.
'Lamia!' he cried – and no soft-toned reply.
The many heard, and the loud revelry
Grew hush; the stately music no more breathes;
The myrtle sickened in a thousand wreaths.
265   By faint degrees, voice, lute, and pleasure ceased;
A deadly silence step by step increased,
Until it seemed a horrid presence there,
And not a man but felt the terror in his hair.
'Lamia!' he shrieked; and nothing but the shriek
270   With its sad echo did the silence break.
'Begone, foul dream!' he cried, gazing again
In the bride's face, where now no azure vein
Wandered on fair-spaced temples; no soft bloom
Misted the cheek; no passion to illume
275   The deep-recessèd vision. All was blight;
Lamia, no longer fair, there sat a deadly white.
'Shut, shut those juggling eyes, thou ruthless man!
Turn them aside, wretch! or the righteous ban
Of all the Gods, whose dreadful images
280   Here represent their shadowy presences,
May pierce them on the sudden with the thorn
Of painful blindness; leaving thee forlorn,
In trembling dotage to the feeblest fright
Of conscience, for their long offended might,
285   For all thine impious proud-heart sophistries,
Unlawful magic, and enticing lies.
Corinthians! look upon that grey-beard wretch!
Mark how, possessed, his lashless eyelids stretch
Around his demon eyes! Corinthians, see!

290 My sweet bride withers at their potency.'
'Fool!' said the sophist, in an undertone
Gruff with contempt; which a death-nighing moan
From Lycius answered, as heart-struck and lost,
He sank supine beside the aching ghost.
295 'Fool! Fool!' repeated he, while his eyes still
Relented not, nor moved: 'From every ill
Of life have I preserved thee to this day,
And shall I see thee made a serpent's prey?'
Then Lamia breathed death-breath; the sophist's eye,
300 Like a sharp spear, went through her utterly,
Keen, cruel, perceant, stinging: she, as well
As her weak hand could any meaning tell,
Motioned him to be silent; vainly so,
He looked and looked again a level – *No!*
305 'A Serpent!' echoed he; no sooner said,
Than with a frightful scream she vanishèd:
And Lycius' arms were empty of delight,
As were his limbs of life, from that same night.
On the high couch he lay! – his friends came round –
310 Supported him – no pulse, or breath they found,
And, in its marriage robe, the heavy body wound.

To Autumn

I
Season of mists and mellow fruitfulness,
   Close bosom-friend of the maturing sun,
Conspiring with him how to load and bless
   With fruit the vines that round the thatch-eves run;
5 To bend with apples the mossed cottage-trees,
   And fill all fruit with ripeness to the core;
     To swell the gourd, and plump the hazel shells

With a sweet kernel; to set budding more,
  And still more, later flowers for the bees,
10   Until they think warm days will never cease,
      For Summer has o'er-brimmed their clammy cells.

II
Who hath not seen thee oft amid thy store?
  Sometimes whoever seeks abroad may find
Thee sitting carelessly on a granary floor,
15   Thy hair soft-lifted by the winnowing wind;
Or on a half-reaped furrow sound asleep,
    Drowsed with the fume of poppies, while thy hook
      Spares the next swath and all its twinèd flowers;
And sometimes like a gleaner thou dost keep
20   Steady thy laden head across a brook;
    Or by a cider-press, with patient look,
      Thou watchest the last oozings hours by hours.

III
Where are the songs of Spring? Ay, where are they?
  Think not of them, thou hast thy music too –
25   While barrèd clouds bloom the soft-dying day,
    And touch the stubble-plains with rosy hue:
Then in a wailful choir the small gnats mourn
    Among the river sallows, borne aloft
      Or sinking as the light wind lives or dies;
30 And full-grown lambs loud bleat from hilly bourn;
    Hedge-crickets sing; and now with treble soft
    The red-breast whistles from a garden-croft;
      And gathering swallows twitter in the skies.

The Fall of Hyperion: A Dream

Canto I

Fanatics have their dreams, wherewith they weave
A paradise for a sect; the savage too
From forth the loftiest fashion of his sleep
Guesses at Heaven: pity these have not
5   Traced upon vellum or wild Indian leaf
The shadows of melodious utterance.
But bare of laurel they live, dream, and die;
For Poesy alone can tell her dreams,
With the fine spell of words alone can save
10 Imagination from the sable charm
And dumb enchantment. Who alive can say
'Thou art no Poet – mayst not tell thy dreams'?
Since every man whose soul is not a clod
Hath visions, and would speak, if he had loved,
15 And been well nurtured in his mother tongue.
Whether the dream now purposed to rehearse
Be Poet's or Fanatic's will be known
When this warm scribe my hand is in the grave.

Methought I stood where trees of every clime,
20 Palm, myrtle, oak, and sycamore, and beech,
With plantain, and spice-blossoms, made a screen –
In neighbourhood of fountains, by the noise
Soft-showering in mine ears, and, by the touch
Of scent, not far from roses. Turning round,
25 I saw an arbour with a drooping roof
Of trellis vines, and bells, and larger blooms,
Like floral censers, swinging light in air;
Before its wreathèd doorway, on a mound
Of moss, was spread a feast of summer fruits,

30   Which, nearer seen, seemed refuse of a meal
       By angel tasted, or our Mother Eve;
       For empty shells were scattered on the grass,
       And grape-stalks but half bare, and remnants more,
       Sweet-smelling, whose pure kinds I could not know.
35   Still was more plenty than the fabled horn
       Thrice emptied could pour forth at banqueting
       For Proserpine returned to her own fields,
       Where the white heifers low. And appetite
       More yearning than on earth I ever felt
40   Growing within, I ate deliciously;
       And, after not long, thirsted, for thereby
       Stood a cool vessel of transparent juice,
       Sipped by the wandered bee, the which I took,
       And, pledging all the mortals of the world,
45   And all the dead whose names are in our lips,
       Drank. That full draught is parent of my theme.
       No Asian poppy, nor elixir fine
       Of the soon-fading jealous Caliphat;
       No poison gendered in close monkish cell,
50   To thin the scarlet conclave of old men,
       Could so have rapt unwilling life away.
       Among the fragrant husks and berries crushed,
       Upon the grass I struggled hard against
       The domineering potion; but in vain –
55   The cloudy swoon came on, and down I sunk,
       Like a Silenus on an antique vase.
       How long I slumbered 'tis a chance to guess.
       When sense of life returned, I started up
       As if with wings; but the fair trees were gone,
60   The mossy mound and arbour were no more.
       I looked around upon the carvèd sides
       Of an old sanctuary with roof august,
       Builded so high, it seemed that filmèd clouds

Might spread beneath, as o'er the stars of heaven.
65 So old the place was, I remembered none
The like upon the earth: what I had seen
Of grey cathedrals, buttressed walls, rent towers,
The superannuations of sunk realms,
Or Nature's rocks toiled hard in waves and winds,
70 Seemed but the faulture of decrepit things
To that eternal domèd monument.
Upon the marble at my feet there lay
Store of strange vessels and large draperies,
Which needs had been of dyed asbestos wove,
75 Or in that place the moth could not corrupt,
So white the linen; so, in some, distinct
Ran imageries from a sombre loom.
All in a mingled heap confused there lay
Robes, golden tongs, censer and chafing-dish,
80 Girdles, and chains, and holy jewelleries –

Turning from these with awe, once more I raised
My eyes to fathom the space every way –
The embossèd roof, the silent massy range
Of columns north and south, ending in mist
85 Of nothing, then to eastward, where black gates
Were shut against the sunrise evermore.
Then to the west I looked, and saw far off
An Image, huge of feature as a cloud,
At level of whose feet an altar slept,
90 To be approached on either side by steps,
And marble balustrade, and patient travail
To count with toil the innumerable degrees.
Towards the altar sober-paced I went,
Repressing haste, as too unholy there;
95 And, coming nearer, saw beside the shrine
One ministering; and there arose a flame.

When in mid-May the sickening East wind
Shifts sudden to the south, the small warm rain
Melts out the frozen incense from all flowers,
100 And fills the air with so much pleasant health
That even the dying man forgets his shroud –
Even so that lofty sacrificial fire,
Sending forth Maian incense, spread around
Forgetfulness of everything but bliss,
105 And clouded all the altar with soft smoke,
From whose white fragrant curtains thus I heard
Language pronounced: 'If thou canst not ascend
These steps, die on that marble where thou art.
Thy flesh, near cousin to the common dust,
110 Will parch for lack of nutriment – thy bones
Will wither in few years, and vanish so
That not the quickest eye could find a grain
Of what thou now art on that pavement cold.
The sands of thy short life are spent this hour,
115 And no hand in the universe can turn
Thy hourglass, if these gummèd leaves be burnt
Ere thou canst mount up these immortal steps.'
I heard, I looked: two senses both at once,
So fine, so subtle, felt the tyranny
120 Of that fierce threat, and the hard task proposed.
Prodigious seemed the toil; the leaves were yet
Burning – when suddenly a palsied chill
Struck from the pavèd level up my limbs,
And was ascending quick to put cold grasp
125 Upon those streams that pulse beside the throat.
I shrieked; and the sharp anguish of my shriek
Stung my own ears – I strove hard to escape
The numbness, strove to gain the lowest step.
Slow, heavy, deadly was my pace: the cold
130 Grew stifling, suffocating, at the heart;

And when I clasped my hands I felt them not.
One minute before death, my iced foot touched
The lowest stair; and as it touched, life seemed
To pour in at the toes: I mounted up,
135 As once fair Angels on a ladder flew
From the green turf to Heaven. 'Holy Power,'
Cried I, approaching near the hornèd shrine,
'What am I that should so be saved from death?
What am I that another death come not
140 To choke my utterance sacrilegious, here?'
Then said the veilèd shadow: 'Thou hast felt
What 'tis to die and live again before
Thy fated hour. That thou hadst power to do so
Is thy own safety; thou hast dated on
145 Thy doom.' 'High Prophetess,' said I, 'purge off,
Benign, if so it please thee, my mind's film.'
'None can usurp this height,' returned that shade,
'But those to whom the miseries of the world
Are misery, and will not let them rest.
150 All else who find a haven in the world,
Where they may thoughtless sleep away their days,
If by a chance into this fane they come,
Rot on the pavement where thou rotted'st half.'
'Are there not thousands in the world,' said I,
155 Encouraged by the sooth voice of the shade,
'Who love their fellows even to the death;
Who feel the giant agony of the world;
And more, like slaves to poor humanity,
Labour for mortal good? I sure should see
160 Other men here: but I am here alone.'
'They whom thou spak'st of are no visionaries,'
Rejoined that voice – 'They are no dreamers weak,
They seek no wonder but the human face;
No music but a happy-noted voice –

165   They come not here, they have no thought to come –
      And thou art here, for thou art less than they –
      What benefit canst thou do, or all thy tribe,
      To the great world? Thou art a dreaming thing,
      A fever of thyself. Think of the Earth;
170   What bliss even in hope is there for thee?
      What haven? Every creature hath its home;
      Every sole man hath days of joy and pain,
      Whether his labours be sublime or low –
      The pain alone; the joy alone; distinct:
175   Only the dreamer venoms all his days,
      Bearing more woe than all his sins deserve.
      Therefore, that happiness be somewhat shared,
      Such things as thou art are admitted oft
      Into like gardens thou didst pass erewhile,
180   And suffered in these temples; for that cause
      Thou standest safe beneath this statue's knees.'
      'That I am favoured for unworthiness,
      By such propitious parley medicined
      In sickness not ignoble, I rejoice –
185   Ay, and could weep for love of such award.'
      So answered I, continuing, 'If it please,
      Majestic shadow, tell me: sure not all
      Those melodies sung into the world's ear
      Are useless: sure a poet is a sage,
190   A humanist, physician to all men.
      That I am none I feel, as vultures feel
      They are no birds when eagles are abroad.
      What am I then? Thou spakest of my tribe:
      What tribe?' – The tall shade veiled in drooping white
195   Then spake, so much more earnest, that the breath
      Moved the thin linen folds that drooping hung
      About a golden censer from the hand
      Pendent. – 'Art thou not of the dreamer tribe?

     The poet and the dreamer are distinct,
200 Diverse, sheer opposite, antipodes.
     The one pours out a balm upon the world,
     The other vexes it.' Then shouted I,
     Spite of myself, and with a Pythia's spleen,
     'Apollo! faded, far-flown Apollo!
205 Where is thy misty pestilence to creep
     Into the dwellings, through the door crannies,
     Of all mock lyrists, large self-worshippers
     And careless hectorers in proud bad verse.
     Though I breathe death with them it will be life
210 To see them sprawl before me into graves.
     Majestic shadow, tell me where I am,
     Whose altar this; for whom this incense curls;
     What image this, whose face I cannot see,
     For the broad marble knees; and who thou art,
215 Of accent feminine, so courteous?'

     Then the tall shade, in drooping linens veiled,
     Spake out, so much more earnest, that her breath
     Stirred the thin folds of gauze that drooping hung
     About a golden censer from her hand
220 Pendent; and by her voice I knew she shed
     Long-treasured tears. 'This temple, sad and lone,
     Is all spared from the thunder of a war
     Foughten long since by giant hierarchy
     Against rebellion; this old image here,
225 Whose carvèd features wrinkled as he fell,
     Is Saturn's; I Moneta, left supreme
     Sole priestess of his desolation.'
     I had no words to answer, for my tongue,
     Useless, could find about its roofèd home
230 No syllable of a fit majesty
     To make rejoinder to Moneta's mourn.

There was a silence, while the altar's blaze
Was fainting for sweet food: I looked thereon,
And on the pavèd floor, where nigh were piled
235   Faggots of cinnamon, and many heaps
Of other crispèd spice-wood – then again
I looked upon the altar, and its horns
Whitened with ashes, and its languorous flame,
And then upon the offerings again;
240   And so by turns – till sad Moneta cried:
'The sacrifice is done, but not the less
Will I be kind to thee for thy goodwill.
My power, which to me is still a curse,
Shall be to thee a wonder; for the scenes
245   Still swooning vivid through my globèd brain,
With an electral changing misery,
Thou shalt with those dull mortal eyes behold,
Free from all pain, if wonder pain thee not.'
As near as an immortal's spherèd words
250   Could to a mother's soften, were these last:
But yet I had a terror of her robes,
And chiefly of the veils, that from her brow
Hung pale, and curtained her in mysteries
That made my heart too small to hold its blood.
255   This saw that Goddess, and with sacred hand
Parted the veils. Then saw I a wan face,
Not pined by human sorrows, but bright-blanched
By an immortal sickness which kills not;
It works a constant change, which happy death
260   Can put no end to; deathwards progressing
To no death was that visage; it had passed
The lily and the snow; and beyond these
I must not think now, though I saw that face –
But for her eyes I should have fled away.
265   They held me back, with a benignant light,

Soft-mitigated by divinest lids
Half-closed, and visionless entire they seemed
Of all external things – they saw me not,
But in blank splendour beamed like the mild moon,
270   Who comforts those she sees not, who knows not
What eyes are upward cast. As I had found
A grain of gold upon the mountain's side,
And twinged with avarice strained out my eyes
To search its sullen entrails rich with ore,
275   So at the view of sad Moneta's brow
I ached to see what things the hollow brain
Behind enwombèd; what high tragedy
In the dark secret chambers of her skull
Was acting, that could give so dread a stress
280   To her cold lips, and fill with such a light
Her planetary eyes; and touch her voice
With such a sorrow – 'Shade of Memory!'
Cried I, with act adorant at her feet,
'By all the gloom hung round thy fallen house,
285   By this last temple, by the golden age,
By great Apollo, thy dear foster child,
And by thyself, forlorn divinity,
The pale Omega of a withered race,
Let me behold, according as thou said'st,
290   What in thy brain so ferments to and fro.'
No sooner had this conjuration passed
My devout lips, than side by side we stood
(Like a stunt bramble by a solemn pine)
Deep in the shady sadness of a vale,
295   Far sunken from the healthy breath of morn,
Far from the fiery noon and eve's one star.
Onward I looked beneath the gloomy boughs,
And saw, what first I thought an image huge,
Like to the image pedestalled so high

300 In Saturn's temple. Then Moneta's voice
    Came brief upon mine ear: 'So Saturn sat
    When he had lost his realms.' Whereon there grew
    A power within me of enormous ken
    To see as a God sees, and take the depth
305 Of things as nimbly as the outward eye
    Can size and shape pervade. The lofty theme
    At those few words hung vast before my mind,
    With half-unravelled web. I set myself
    Upon an eagle's watch, that I might see,
310 And seeing ne'er forget. No stir of life
    Was in this shrouded vale, not so much air
    As in zoning of a summer's day
    Robs not one light seed from the feathered grass,
    But where the dead leaf fell there did it rest.
315 A stream went voiceless by, still deadened more
    By reason of the fallen divinity
    Spreading more shade; the Naiad 'mid her reeds
    Pressed her cold finger closer to her lips.
    Along the margin-sand large footmarks went
320 No farther than to where old Saturn's feet
    Had rested, and there slept – how long a sleep!
    Degraded, cold, upon the sodden ground
    His old right hand lay nerveless, listless, dead,
    Unsceptered; and his realmless eyes were closed,
325 While his bowed head seemed listening to the Earth,
    His ancient mother, for some comfort yet.

Notes

On First Looking into Chapman's Homer

George Chapman (1559–1634) published a translation of Homer's *Iliad* and *Odyssey*. Keats's friend, Charles Cowden Clarke, read it with him one evening, and Keats returned to his lodgings in Dean Street by dawn to write this sonnet by five o'clock the following evening. It was published a few weeks later in *The Examiner*, on 1 December 1816.

Petrarchan in construction, it is made up of an octet (eight lines) and a sestet (six lines). The former considers Keats's reading experiences before Chapman, and the latter his reading experiences since.

1 **realms of gold** both the world of the imagination and the world of poetry. The poet insists that he has read widely and well.
2 **goodly** large.
3 This alludes to the voyages of Odysseus, Homer's hero in the *Odyssey*.
4 **bards** poets.
  fealty loyalty or allegiance, originally between a tenant and his feudal lord.
  Apollo Greek god of poetry and music. The poet has now turned to consider himself as the creator of poetry, not just the reader of it.
6 **deep-browed** intellectual.
  demesne realm.
7 **pure serene** derived from the Latin *serenum*, meaning the pure air from a clear sky. What is Keats saying about the importance of poetry here?
9 **Then** a conjunction that moves the poem in a slightly different direction, in order to separate the octave and sestet.

10 **swims into his ken** comes into his sight. Note that the verb
swims is just one example of the water imagery in this poem.
11 **stout Cortez** the brave Hernando Cortez, a Spanish explorer.
However, in fact it was Vasco Nunez de Balboa (1475–1519)
who first saw the Pacific Ocean in 1513 and claimed it for
Spain.
14 **Darien** a mountain range running the length of the isthmus
of Darien in Central America. Today, this is in Panama.

Keen, Fitful Gusts

Published in 1817, this sonnet refers to Keats's stay in Leigh
Hunt's cottage in Hampstead. Their wide-ranging discussions
were said to have included the works of Petrarch (1304–1374)
and John Milton (1608–1674).

12 **Lycid** *Lycidus*, a pastoral elegy by Milton. In 1645, when
editing his poems, Milton wrote of the elegy 'bewail[ing] a
learned Friend, unfortunately drowned... on the Irish Seas,
1637'.
13 **Laura** the subject of many of Petrarch's sonnets. It was said
to have been on 6 April 1327, in the Church of St Clare, that
the Italian poet Francesco Petrarca (known as Petrarch), fell in
love with this young woman – whose identity remains
unknown. His love remained unrequited, but endured even
after her death.

To my Brothers

In November 1816, Keats wrote this sonnet on his brother Tom's
birthday. All three brothers were living in the same house in
London.

3 **household gods**   the gods of the hearth, particular to each Roman household.
7 **lore**   knowledge.
voluble   fluent.
8 **condoles**   expresses sympathy.

To Haydon

This is a sonnet that Keats wrote in November 1816, having met the painter Benjamin Robert Haydon (1786–1846) earlier that year.

1 **Great spirits**   Benjamin Haydon, William Wordsworth and Leigh Hunt, each of whom is mentioned in the sonnet.
sojourning   staying temporarily.
2 **He of the cloud**   Wordsworth, the Romantic poet.
cataract   a large waterfall or rapids.
3 **Helvellyn**   the mountain in Cumbria of which Wordsworth had a view from his home. Haydon painted *Wordsworth Musing Upon Helvellyn*.
4 **Archangel**   principal angel.
5 **He of the rose**   Leigh Hunt, who transformed his prison cell by decorating it with flowered wallpaper.
6 **the chain for Freedom's sake**   a specific reference to Hunt's imprisonment.
8 **Raphael**   name of an an archangel and also a famous Renaissance painter (1483–1520); both are used in tribute to Haydon.
13 This incomplete line has the reader pause for the remaining five syllable beats, in order to dwell on the question posed about the imagination, and to pre-empt the silence demanded in the final line. Originally, Keats had finished the line with *in a distant Mart*: which line do you prefer, and why?

Benjamin Robert Haydon,
the painter who was Keats's
friend

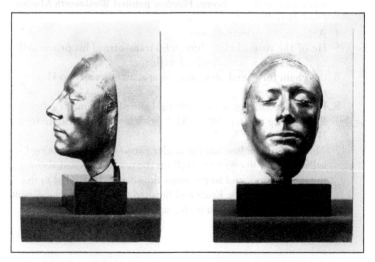

A life mask of Keats made by Haydon in autumn 1816

On the Grasshopper and Cricket

In December 1816, Keats entered into competition with his friend Leigh Hunt, as to who could produce a sonnet on a specific subject in a certain length of time. The result is a nature poem, and its language is simple and straightforward throughout. Note the use of sibilance, which creates a soft and relaxing atmosphere.

4 **mead**   meadow.
9 This line is almost a direct repetition of the opening line. The poet seems to be suggesting that poetry and nature are inextricably linked.

On the Sea

While staying on the Isle of Wight in 1817, Keats wrote this sonnet – and included it in a letter to John Hamilton Reynolds. Structurally, it is written in the same form as *On First Looking into Chapman's Homer*, but most critics agree that it does not compare in terms of magnitude of feeling. The main thrust of the poem is to describe the sea as both impressive and subtle in its effects.

3 **Gluts**   supplies excessively.
4 **Hecate**   an ancient, pre-Olympian Greek goddess of fertility, who received divine powers from Zeus in order to preside over heaven, earth and the ocean. As earth-goddess, she later became more well known for her association with the underworld, ghosts and sorcery.
9 **Oh ye!**   the sestet opens with an invocation to those who need the sea for comfort. The invocation is repeated in line 11, and the notion of the healing powers of the sea continues to the sonnet's close.
   vexed   annoyed.
11 **dinned with uproar rude**   Keats captures the sound effect with the use of onomatopoeia.
14 **quired**   sang as part of a choir.

Endymion

Endymion is composed of four books of about 1,000 lines each. Written in 1817 and published in 1818, it never attracted very much in the way of praise, but has always been considered of significance not least because it charts the young poet's development.

It is based on the Greek myth of the shepherd, Endymion, who became immortal because of his love for the moon goddess, Diana or Cynthia. Keats wrote of his poetic endeavours to his sister, Fanny, while he was staying with Benjamin Bailey in Oxford:

> Perhaps you might like to know what I am writing about – I will tell you –
>
> Many Years ago there was a young handsome Shepherd who fed his flocks on a Mountain's Side called Latmus – he was a very contemplative sort of a Person and lived solitry among the trees and Plains little thinking – that such a beautiful Creature as the Moon was growing mad in Love with him – However so it was; and when he was asleep on the Grass, she used to come down from heaven and admire him excessively [for] a long time; and at last could not refrain from carying him away in her arms to the top of that high Mountain Latmus while he was a dreaming – but I dare say [you] have read this and all the other beautiful Tales which have come down from the ancient times of that beautiful Greece.
>
> 10 September 1817

19 **musk-rose**   a white rambling rose with a smell of musk.
20 **dooms**   destinies.

Lines 232–306

Composed on 26 April 1817. Pan is the son of Mercury and the god of universal nature; these lines are spoken by a priest to the god on behalf of shepherds everywhere.

236 **hamadryads**   wood-nymphs, said to die with the tree they inhabit.

241 **pipy hemlock**   the tall, hollow pipes of the poisonous hemlock plant.

243 **Syrinx**   in Greek mythology, a nymph who was changed into a reed in order to escape the amorous advances of Pan. It was out of this reed that Pan's famous musical pipes were made.

247 **turtles**   turtle-doves.

248 **myrtles**   evergreen shrubs with white flowers, sacred to Venus, and her emblem as the goddess of love.

252 **foredoom**   anticipate, foreshadow.

253 **girted**   striped.

254 **leas**   meadows.

256 **chuckling**   clucking.

258 **pent up butterflies**   butterflies in their chrysalis.

261 **pine**   Pan's emblem.

263 **faun**   in Roman mythology, a rural deity, represented as a man with a goat's ears, horns, tail and hind legs.
satyr   in Greek mythology, a goat-like sylvan deity who followed the god of hedonism, Dionysus.

267 **maw**   mouth, throat or stomach.

272 **Naiads**   water-nymphs.

281 **Winder of the horn**   the horn-blower.

282 **routing**   using the snout for digging.

290 **Dryope**   Pan was said to have been born of Dryope and Hermes.

295 **bourne**   boundary.

296 **leaven**   yeast.

298 **ethereal**   divine.

305 **paean**   hymn of praise.

306 **Mount Lycean**   a mountain in Arcadia, sacred to Pan.

Lines 777–842

Keats wrote to his friend John Taylor about the following lines, outlining his thoughts on 'a kind of Pleasure Thermometer' that set out for him 'the gradations of Happiness', moving his imagination to a greater truth (30 January 1818). Keats considered the four degrees of happiness to be the enjoyment that comes from nature, music, friendship, and passion. Endymion himself is the narrator of this section of verse.

777 **becks** beckons.
779 **essence** a reference to the 'thing of beauty'.
780 **alchemized** transformed, in much the same way as alchemy was believed to change base metals into gold.
786 **Aeolian magic** the sound of the god of the wind, Aeolus, on his harp.
787 **enclouded** obscure.
791 **clarions** trumpets.
 bruit proclaim.
792 **giant battle** the war between the Titans and the Olympians (the backdrop to *Hyperion*).
794 **Orpheus** a figure from myth who was taught to play the lyre skilfully by his father, Apollo. So moving was his music that it was said to be able to influence nature.
806 **orbèd** spherical.
808 **genders** engenders, creates.
814 **pith** centre.
815 **pelican brood** according to legend, the pelican feeds her young with her own blood.
816 **unsating** unsatisfying.
817 **van** front – a metaphor to suggest those at the front of an army on the attack.
819 **winnow** separate; this is a reference to separating the wheat from the *chaff* (820) at harvest time.
823 **elysium** for the Greeks, that place where total happiness is experienced.
825 **ardent listlessness** a trance-like state.
837 **mail** scales.
838 **dower** inheritance.
839 **runnels** small streams.

On Sitting Down to Read *King Lear* Once Again

Keats wrote this sonnet in January 1818. At the time, he was planning *Hyperion*, a poem that also deals with tragedy.

1 **Romance**   personifying romance, the poet rejects his own brand of escapist poetry, writing in order to commit himself to the mood of *King Lear*.
2 **Syren**   in Greek mythology, a sea nymph whose singing was said to lure sailors to crash on the rocks. Note that Keats personifies this and *Queen* in the same line, both with reference to romance.
7 **burn through**   the reading of the Shakespeare play is metaphorically likened to dealing with fire, an image picked up in the final couplet.
  assay   attempt.
9 **Albion**   the backdrop for *King Lear*; the ancient name for England.
14 **Phoenix**   a legendary Arabian bird, believed to set fire to itself and rise from the ashes every 500 years.
  The final line contains an extra two syllables, and so breaks the established pattern of regular pentameters (lines of ten syllables). This emphasizes the poet's longing for freedom, which he will achieve through reading, and this is made even more definite by the use of a rhyming couplet.

When I have Fears

Written in 1818, this sonnet focuses on some of Keats's major themes: time, death and ambition. It follows the Shakespearean sonnet structure, made up of an octave and a sestet with the rhyme scheme *ababcdcdefefgg*, and there is a definite break in content. The first part is full of harvest imagery, linked to the fertility of the poet's imagination, while the second has him accepting the lack of importance of fame in the grander scheme of things. In his own life, Keats was very ambitious, but debilitating illness prevented him from writing from the age of 24. As a result, Keats saw himself as having failed, insisting that the inscription for his headstone be 'Here lies one whose name was writ in water'.

1 **When**   the repetition of this word at the beginning of each quatrain emphasizes the poet's preoccupation with the passing of time.
2 **gleaned**   picked up or out. The paradox is that the poet is both the grain to be harvested (the imagination), and the harvester (producer of poetry). Note the alliteration of the letters 'g' and 'r' in the opening quatrain, subtly reinforcing the importance of these elements.
3 **charactery**   printing or handwriting.
4 **garners**   barn, continuing the harvesting imagery.
9–10 The poet's emotions tell him that both his beloved, and love itself, are short-lived.
11 **faery power**   imaginative force.
12 **shore**   standing on the brink between two worlds – the land and the sea – the poet comes to the realization (through thinking, not emoting) that love and fame are unimportant. Note that the third quatrain is cut short in the twelfth line; why do you think this is significant?

Lines on the Mermaid Tavern

Keats wrote this poem in February 1818 to focus on the legendary Mermaid Tavern, frequented by the most famous of Renaissance writers including Shakespeare and Ben Jonson. A light-hearted poem, its mood is reinforced by the regular eight-syllable couplets.

2 **Elysium**   in Greek mythology, the dwelling place of the blessed after death.

7 **fruits of Paradise** heaven.

12 **bowse** get drunk; an eighteenth-century word that eventually became 'booze'.

16 **astrologer** who saw the likes of Shakespeare and Jonson still enjoying themselves at another such drinking establishment in the heavens.

17 **sheepskin** parchment.

23–6 The opening refrain is repeated at the close of the poem, a rhetorical question adding to the whimsical tone.

Isabella, or The Pot of Basil

Written in 1818, this poem is based upon Giovanni Boccaccio's story of Isabella and Lorenzo. The stanzaic form was new to Keats. It is the Italian *ottava rima* – consisting of eight iambic pentameters (lines of ten syllables, mainly in the pattern of an unstressed followed by a stressed syllable), with the rhyme scheme *abababcc*.

2 **a young palmer in Love's eye** a young pilgrim with love in mind.

21 **vespers** evening prayers.

34 Love should reflect the bloom of the rose; instead, the cheek is pallid.

39 **looks speak love-laws** love shows itself in Isabella's face.

46 **Fevered his high conceit** the thought of Isabella becoming his bride makes Lorenzo break out in a fever; as yet, his love is unrequited.

62 **fear** make afraid.

64 **shrive** confess.

70 **dewy** fresh.

75 **close** secretly.

95–6 Ariadne was deserted by Theseus, despite aiding him in his bid to kill the Minotaur.

99 **Dido** in Virgil's *Aeneid*, Dido is deserted by Aeneas, and commits suicide. Aeneas meets her again on his visit to the underworld.

101–2 These lines foreshadow Lorenzo's death and burial in the forests.

103 **almsmen** men who pray for dead people's souls.

107 **swelt** swelter, sweat.

108 **torchèd** illuminated by torches.

113 **Ceylon diver** the diver whose hearing was often affected when plummeting to great depths in search of pearls.

120 **peel** strip the skin.

124 **lazar stairs** 'lazar' is an archaic word for leper; the stairs are where those with leprosy sit to beg.

131 **close** secretive.
      land inspired Palestine.

132 **Paled in** fenced in.

136 **Spanish, Tuscan, and Malay** languages useful in commerce.

140 **Egypt's pest** blindness; relating to the plague of darkness set upon the Egyptians in Exodus 10:21–3.

145 **Boccaccio** Giovanni Boccaccio (1313–1375), well-known Italian poet, famous for his collection of stories known as *The Decameron*.

146 **forgiving boon** the ability to forgive.

147 **myrtles** an evergreen shrub or tree, considered to be a symbol of love.

150 **gittern** a stringed instrument.

155 **assail** attempt.

158 **gone** departed, dead.

159 **stead** serve.

163 **unconfines** displays.

168 **olive-trees** only the very wealthy would have an orchard of olive trees. It is clear that Isabella's brothers want her to marry for money.

176 **and there bury him** the brevity of the clause complements the dramatic brevity of the act.

184 **while cold is in the skies** before the sun heats the day.

186 **the Apennine** an Italian mountain range.

187–8 The sun, drying the dew on the briar, is metaphorically said to be counting beads on a rosary. This reference is ironic, since its religious overtones belie the irreligious intentions of the brothers.

195 **matin-song** morning song.

203 **what if I should lose thee**   this foreshadows Lorenzo's death.

209 **murdered**   again, this anticipates Lorenzo's death before it happens.

210 **Arno**   the river that flows through Florence.

213 **freshets**   streams caused by the sudden overflowing of a river. The pause or caesura here emphasizes the transition from the natural scenery to the unnatural act of the brothers.

221 **break-covert**   breaking free, in anticipation of slaughter.

236 **luxury**   sentiment.

242 **single**   love is the only feeling that her heart can contain.

243 **golden hour**   the hour of Lorenzo's return.

248 **rude**   hard, rough.

249–55 A description of the decline of nature in autumn, in anticipation of the tragedy to follow.

259 **dungeon climes**   dreadful places (where Lorenzo may have been detained).

262 **Hinnom's vale**   the valley in 2 Chronicles 28:3 where idol-worshippers sacrificed their children.

268 **feathered pall**   death.

287 **under-song**   echoing melody.

288 **sepulchral**   of the graveyard.

292 **woof**   pattern.

320 **essence**   being, soul.

344 **forest-hearse**   place of burial in the forest.

347 **champaign**   countryside.

393 **Persèan sword**   according to myth, Perseus was able to perform many heroic feats with his sword, including the decapitation of the Gorgon, Medusa.

398 **impersonate**   embodied.

401–8 Note all the images of both beauty and repulsion in this stanza.

412 **serpent-pipe**   a distillation pipe, curved like a snake.

432 **leafits**   small leaves.

433–8 Isabella's impending death is foreshadowed in the apostrophes to various spirits.

442 **Melpomene**   the tragic muse.

451 **Baälites of pelf**   heathens who worship the money god.

467 **chapel-shrift**   confession at chapel.

Old Meg

Written in July 1818, when Keats was travelling with Charles Brown in Scotland, 'Old Meg' tells the story of Meg Merrilies, a character in Walter Scott's *Guy Mannering*. The poem is written in ballad form (apart from the final six lines), with each quatrain rhyming at the second and fourth lines. Such regularity and simplicity highlights the notion of poverty, both in terms of its daily grind and its basic pleasures.

    5 **swart** archaic word for dark-hued.

  25 **Margaret Queen** Margaret of Anjou, the brave wife of Henry VI, fifteenth-century King of England. She fought her husband's cause in the Wars of the Roses.

  26 **Amazon** according to legend, a race of female warriors. They needed men only to help produce the next generation, and were famous for cauterizing one breast in order to better wield their bows in battle.

  28 **chip-hat** a hat made of woven strips of wood.

25–30 The comparisons of this final stanza make Old Meg appear noble, despite her poverty, and the final two lines add both pathos and further realism to the poem.

Hyperion: A Fragment

Hyperion is an unfinished poem, composed between late September and early December 1818, and abandoned completely in the spring of the following year. Consisting of three books, the narrative is based upon the myth of the Titans – the gods who had Saturn as their leader – and their defeat. Keats chooses to focus upon the god Hyperion, who was to be overthrown by Apollo.

Book I

3 **eve's one star**   the evening star, Venus.

4 **grey-haired Saturn**   the leader of the defeated Titans, and brother to Hyperion. The poem opens *in medias res* (in the middle of the story). Saturn has been defeated by his renegade son, Jupiter.

13 **Naiad**   water-nymph.

18 **nerveless**   weak.

23 **one**   Thea, wife of Hyperion and sister of Saturn.

27 **Amazon**   according to Greek myth, one of a race of female warriors.

28 **pigmy**   dwarf.

29 **Achilles**   in Greek myth, he was the foremost of the warriors in the siege against Troy.

30 **Ixion's wheel**   in Greek legend, Ixion was the Thessalian king punished by Zeus for his love of Hera by being bound to a perpetually moving wheel in Hades.

31 **Memphian sphinx**   a large statue, part animal, part woman, which stands in Memphis, Egypt.

39 **vanward**   first. This likens calamity to the clouds building before a storm, followed by the mass of clouds itself and then the storm – the latter being compared to an artillery preparing (*labouring up*, 41) when the opposing army advances.

51 **To**   in comparison with.

59 **hoary**   white-haired.

60 **conscious of the new command**   the new thunderer is Jupiter.

63 **our once serene domain**   the golden age of Saturn's rule.

83–4 The moon has completed four quarters.

86 This simile compares the gods to huge rocks.

87 **couchant**   reclining.

93 **palsied**   trembling.

94 **horrid**   bristling.
   aspen-malady   shaking like the leaves of an aspen tree.

95 Thea is both the sister and the third wife of Hyperion.

101 **diadem**   crown.

102 **Peers**   appears.
   front   forehead.

105 **nervous**   vigorous or forceful.

107–8 Jupiter has taken firm control of all the planets.
114 According to legend, the Titans relied upon their sense of self for power.
117 **eterne** eternal.
118 **lorn** deprived.
129 **gold clouds metropolitan** the clouds are the gods' golden realm, or metropolis.
137 **Druid locks** long hair.
145 **Chaos** the earth is said to have been created out of chaos.
146 **Olympus** the mountain that was the home of Jupiter and the other deities.
147 **The rebel three** Jupiter, Neptune and Pluto, Saturn's sons.
150 **our friends** the race of the Titans.
152 **covert** secret place.
166 **orbèd fire** the sun, of which Hyperion is the god.
171 **gloom-bird** owl, a bird whose night screeching is associated with death.
173 **passing-bell** death-knell.
175 **portioned** proportioned.
176–82 The imagery denoting Hyperion's palace suggests that it is both Roman and Egyptian in design.
181 **Aurorian** rosy; linked to Aurora, the goddess of the dawn.
197 **minions** favourites.
204 **slope** downward sloping.
206 **tubes** of a musical instrument, such as an organ or trumpet.
207 **Zephyrs** west winds.
209 **vermeil** red.
216 **Hours** Horae, the gods who attended the changing of the seasons.
221 **cupola** dome.
226 **curb** restraint.
232 **essence** essential being.
238 **fanes** temples.
239 **lucent** shining.
246 **Tellus** mother of the Titans, married to her brother Saturn. Said to be the first being to be born of Chaos, she was protector of the earth and therefore marriage, fertility and death.
249 **infant thunderer, rebel Jove** Jove, or Jupiter, had thrown thunderbolts when attempting to usurp his father Saturn's throne.

266 **portals** gateways.

274 **colure** a great circle on the celestial sphere, passing either through the celestial poles and the equinoxes or through the poles and the solstices.

276 **nadir** the opposite of the *zenith* – the lowest point in the heavens.

277 **hieroglyphics old** signs of the zodiac.

282 **swart** black.

284 **argent** silver.

290 **Fain** gladly.

298 **demesnes** domains.

299 **bright Titan** Hyperion.

302 **rack of clouds** a mass of clouds.

307 **Coelus** father of the Titans, overthrown by his son, Hyperion.

311 **the powers** Coelus and Terra, the parents of the Titans.

322 **son against his sire** Jupiter's war against Saturn.

323 **first-born** Saturn.

326 **wox** became.

338 **an evident God** the philosophy being that Saturn is a tangible being, whereas Coelus is the sky, and notionally a mere place.

343–4 **in the van/Of circumstance** take immediate action.

344–5 **seize the arrow's barb/Before the tense string murmur** the emphasis is, once again, upon seizing the initiative, with the image suggesting that a warrior should shoot an arrow before the enemy shoots his.

Book II

4 **Cybele** Saturn's wife.

5 **insulting light** the light would remind the Titans of their loss of power, insulting them still further.

19–20 All gods and Titans, with the exception of *Dolor*, considered to be the personification of grief.

28 **sanguine** of the blood.
gurge whirlpool.

29 **Mnemosyne** mother of the muses, and one of the Titans. She is searching for Apollo.

30 **Phoebe** the moon goddess.

32 **covert**   shelter.

34 **cirque**   circle.

37 **chancel vault**   the gloomy darkness and the stones are reminiscent of a church.

39 **shroud**   shrouded, hidden in the dark.

41 **Creüs**   Saturn's brother.

44 **Iäpetus**   Saturn's brother.

45 **plashy**   patterned as if splashed with colour.

46 **gorge**   throat.

49 **Cottus**   Saturn's brother.

52 **at horrid working**   glaring in a very menacing fashion.

53 **Asia**   the goddess daughter of Caf, a legendary Persian mountain, and Tellus.

60 **Oxus**   an Asian river.

61 **anchor**   in the Bible, an emblem of hope (Hebrews 6:19).

64 **shelve**   slope.

66 **Enceladus**   a Titan well known for his great strength.

69 **even now**   i.e. in his mind.

70 **that second war**   a war which was probably to have come in another poetic book of the same subject.

73 **Atlas**   a Titan who was made to support the sky upon his shoulders as punishment for rebelling against Jupiter.

74 **Phorcus**   a sea god.
   Gorgons   three winged, monstrous sisters, who had serpents for hair, huge teeth and deadly claws. One look from a Gorgon would turn a man to stone.

75 **Oceanus**   a water god.
   Tethys   married to Oceanus.

77 **Themis**   a Titan.

78 **Ops**   an alternative name for Cybele, Saturn's wife.

86 **horrid**   horrifying.

95 **spleen**   anger.

98 **disanointing poison**   a poison that strips Saturn of his throne.

99 **kept her still**   kept herself still.

128 **silverly**   with a silvery sound.

133 **old spirit-leavèd book**   a fabled text, which supposedly recorded events from the beginning of time.

134 **Uranus**   father of Saturn, and god of the skies.

161 **engine our great wrath**   make our wrath warlike.

165 **astonied** astonished.

167 **God of the Sea** Oceanus.

168 **Sophist and sage** philosopher and wise man.
no Athenian grove Oceanus did not obtain his wisdom
from an Athenian academy.

170 **locks not oozy** Oceanus is not in the water.

176 **ire** anger.

183 **atom-universe** John Dalton had argued in 1801 that all
elements are made up of atoms.

190 'I am Alpha and Omega, the beginning and the ending, saith
the Lord' (Revelation 1:8)

192 **intestine broil** civil war.

196 **its own producer** Chaos.

208 **show beyond** are superior to.

232 **young God of the Seas** Neptune.

244 **posed** feigned.

250 **hectic** feverish, flushed.

274 **bowery strand** sheltered beach.

286 **dove... olive** symbols of peace.

306 **half-glutted** half-filled.

318 **youngling arm** young and inexperienced person.

328 **ether of our enemies** air breathed by our enemies.

329 **crooked stings of fire** lightning flashes.

341 **wingèd thing** the goddess of Victory, Nike, depicted as
having wings.

358 **beetling** overhanging.

365 **Mantled** cloaked.

369–70 Hyperion's brilliance is a great contrast to the Titans' misery.

371 **Numidian curl** the Numidian race, from the north coast of
Africa, were famed for their curly hair.

374–6 **Memnon** son of Aurora, goddess of the dawn, linked to the
colossal statue of Amenophis near Thebes, Egypt. It was
believed that a tune came from his harp when struck by the
sun at dawn and sunset.

386 **eminence** mountain.

Book III

2 **Amazèd**   distracted.

3 **Muse**   the nine muses were the daughters of Jupiter and Mnemosyne, and represented the arts, poetry and science. Keats refers here to the muse of tragedy, Melpomene.

8 **Divinity**   god.

10 **Delphic harp**   Apollo's lyre.

12 **Dorian**   what Keats considered to be a music of 'sad-sweet melody'.

13 **the Father of all verse**   Apollo, god of the sun and of poetry.

23 **Cyclades**   islands in the Aegean Sea, which encircled Delos, Apollo's place of birth.

29 **Giant of the Sun**   Hyperion.

31 **his mother**   Latona.

32 **twin-sister**   Diana.

34 **osiers**   willows.

44 **suffusèd**   tearful.

46 **awful Goddess**   Mnemosyne, who had defected from the side of the Titans to join with Apollo.

51 **mien**   look, presence.

80 **gloomless eyes**   once he hears Mnemosyne, Apollo's gloom leaves him.

92 **liegeless**   without a master.

105 **alarum**   turmoil.

113 **Knowledge enormous**   Apollo's awareness of suffering is what has made him a god.

115 **sovran**   sovereign.

119 **elixir**   a potion that the ancients believed would make man immortal.

136 **Celestial**   looking upon Mnemosyne's face has given Apollo the understanding and ability to become a god once more.

Ode

Written in December 1818, this poem was said by Keats to be 'a sort of rondeau', meaning that its opening lines are repeated at the close as a refrain. Keats did label the poem an ode, and there are obvious links between the structure (seven-syllable couplets) and content of this poem and *Lines on the Mermaid Tavern*.

4 **Double-lived**   in that poets, once dead, achieve immortality through their work.

8 **parle**   talk.

11 **Elysian**   the home of the blessed dead, within Elysium.

12 **Dian**   Diana, the virginal Roman goddess of the moon and the hunt.

36 The poet suggests that poetry is a kind of wisdom, because of the experience that is needed to produce it.

37–40 The repetition (with one significant change) of the opening four lines reinforces the ode's main theme that poets have the chance to live again.

Fancy

Keats wrote this poem in December 1818, and presented to his readers the joy of allowing the 'fancy' to wander at will. It is important to note the difference between the imagination and fancy. While the former is that part of the mind which creates, the fancy is defined as the whimsical part of the imagination. For Keats, fancy is personified as wandering, in order to be allowed to return with the perfect mistress for the poet. However, as always, Keats makes the point that flights of fancy are not to be confused with reality.

16 **ingle**   fire.

17 **sear faggot**   dried-out bundle of sticks.

21 **shoon**   shoes.

24 **Even**   evening.

28 **vassals**   servants.

34 **sward**   grass.

39 **quaff**   drink.

81 **Dulcet-eyed**   pleasant- or sweet-eyed.
Ceres' daughter   Proserpine, the Roman counterpart of Persephone, who was snatched by Pluto and taken to the Underworld against her will.

85 **Hebe** the daughter of Zeus and Hera, Hebe is the Greek goddess of youth.
zone belt.

87 **kirtle** a woman's skirt or dress.

The Eve of St Agnes

Written in early 1819, this poem focuses upon the superstitious belief that, should a girl go to bed without supper on St Agnes's Eve (20 January), her lover will appear before her in a vision.

5 **Beadsman** an archaic word for a person who prays for the soul of his patron.

6 **rosary** a string of beads used to count prayers as they are recited.

7 **censer** incense container.

16 **orat'ries** small rooms for private prayer.

22 **already had his deathbell rung** his destiny is already written.

31 **silver, snarling trumpets** onomatopoeia, used to suggest the sound of the instruments.

37 **argent** silver.

55–6 The half-rhyme of *Madeline* and *pain* adds to the whimsical feel.

58 **sweeping train** a long dress, trailing along the floor.

67 **timbrels** tambourines or small drums.

70 **hoodwinked** deceived.
amort dead (Keats's coinage).

71 **lambs unshorn** St Agnes's emblem is a lamb, and two lambs were blessed at the St Agnes mass.

77 **Buttressed** hidden in the shadows of the church buttress.

81 **in sooth** in truth.

88 **lineage** ancestry.

90 **beldame** an archaic word for an old woman or hag.

92 **wand** walking stick.

95 **bland** soft.

97 **palsied** trembling.

105 **gossip** old woman, confidante.

108 **bier** a platform upon which the corpse, or coffin containing the corpse, is carried to the place of burial.

120–2 Porphyro must produce sheer magic to achieve his aims.

121 **Fays** fairies.

126 **mickle** much.

129 **urchin** a mischievous child.

133 **brook** hold back.

136 A simile that conveys both the image of a thought coming quickly and sexual passion. The rose image will continue throughout the poem.

138 **purple riot** this image is significant on two counts. (1) Porphyro's heart is beating so quickly that the blood is a deeper colour, and (2) the word Porphyro is Greek for purple, and is symbolic of ardour.

143 **deem** judge.

149 **ruffian passion** brutal sexual desire.

153 **beard** defy.

155 **churchyard** i.e. near death.

156 **passing-bell** the death knell, tolled when someone dies.

158 **plaining** complaining, lamenting.

162 **betide her weal or woe** no matter (*betide*) what happens to her, in terms of well-being (*weal*) or misfortune (*woe*).

168–9 Phrases such as *legioned faeries* and *pale enchantment* serve to enhance the romantic atmosphere of the poem.

171 In Arthurian legend, Merlin was a magician to the king. In old age, he was eternally imprisoned in a tree by the woman he loved, to whom he had revealed the secrets of his magic. He *paid his Demon* with his own death.

173 **cates and dainties** delicacies for eating.

174 **tambour frame** a frame for embroidery, shaped like a drum or tambourine.

184 **agèd eyes aghast** eyes wide open with fear. Note that the assonance emphasizes the effect.

188 **amain** exceedingly.

189 **agues** shivering.

190 **balustrade** banister.

193 **missioned** suggests that the supernatural spirit has been commissioned or assigned.

194 **taper** candle.

198 **like ring-dove frayed and fled** a simile suggesting the fearful dove that has flown away.

200 **pallid** lacking colour, wan.

204 **voluble** audible.

206 **tongueless nightingale** in Ovid's *Metamorphoses* (VI 425–675), Philomela is raped by her brother-in-law, Tereus, who then cuts out her tongue so that she cannot speak his name. The gods, in sympathy, change her into a nightingale.

208 **casement high** so begins a beautiful description of a window. This is soon to be contrasted with the incomparable beauties of Madeline.

209 **imag'ries** designs.

211 **quaint device** unusual style.

213 **deep-damasked wings** bold marks on either side of its wings.

214 **heraldries** insignia on arms, displaying a person's or family's genealogy.

215 **emblazoning** splendid heraldic images.

216 **scutcheon** a heraldic shield, displaying a coat-of-arms.

218 **gules** the heraldic word for 'red'.

219 **boon** favour.

221 **amethyst** a semi-precious stone, purple in colour.

222 **glory** halo.

222–5 Note the spiritual register, as Madeline is linked to *a saint* (222) and *a splendid angel* (223), while being fit for *Heaven* (224) and *free from mortal taint* (225).

226 **vespers** evening prayers.

233 **fancy** imagination.

234 **charm** magic.

237 **poppied** poppies contain opium, and so have a soporific effect. Examine this stanza as a whole, and pick out the examples of sibilance that dominate; this technique also conveys the image of sleepiness.

240 **havened** sheltered.

241 **Clasp'd like a missal where swart Paynims pray** clasped like a prayer book shut in the presence of dark pagans.

257 **Morphean amulet** a charm to keep Madeline asleep in order that Porphyro might complete his provisions. In Greek myth, Morpheus is the god of sleep and dreams.

260 **Affray** disturb.

265 **gourd**   melon.

266 **soother**   smoother.

267 **lucent syrups, tinct**   clear syrups tinctured.

268 **argosy**   a ship, or fleet of ships.

269 **Fez**   a city in Morocco associated with sugar.

270 **Samarkand**   a city in Russia famed for its silk.
  Lebanon   a republic in West Asia, on the Mediterranean, renowned for its cedar wood.

276 **seraph**   angel.

277 **eremite**   a Christian hermit.

280 **unnervèd**   weak.

284 **salvers**   trays.

286 **redeem**   free.

288 **woofèd**   woven.

292 **La belle dame sans mercy**   see Keats's poem of the same name.

296 **affrayèd**   alarmed.

303 **witless**   unknown.

311 **pallid, chill, and drear**   words that contrast with the action to follow.

313 **complainings**   laments.

316–24 This stanza describes the sexual consummation of the pair, conveyed in an image of the rose and the violet blending.

323 **Love's alarum**   Cupid's warning.

325 **flaw-blown**   wind-blown.

333 **dove forlorn**   the bird imagery continues, unifying the poem.

335 **for aye thy vassal**   forever your servant.

336 **vermeil**   the colour vermillion is bright red.

342 **infidel**   non-believer.

344 **haggard seeming**   wild appearance.

346 **bloated wassaillers**   revellers who are full of drink.

349 **Rhenish**   wine from the Rhine region in Germany.
  sleepy mead   a sleep-inducing drink fermented from malt and honey.

355 **darkling**   in the dark.

358 **arras**   a tapestry, often used as a wall-hanging.

363 **Porter**   gatekeeper.

366 **an inmate owns**   acknowledges Madeline, an occupant of the house.

377 **aves**   repetitions of the Latin prayer, *Ave Maria* (Hail Mary).

The Eve of St Mark

Written in February 1819, this poem contemplates a superstition connected with St Mark. It was said that on the eve of his saint's day (24 April), a person who watched the church door would see the ghosts of those fated to die in the next year.

  1 **Sabbath-day** Sunday.

  2 **Twice holy** it being also a Saint's day.

 10 **sedge** a grass-like plant with spiky flowers, growing on wet ground.

 12 **aguish** shivering.

 16 **orat'ries** small rooms for private prayer.

 17 **demurest** the most modest and sedate.

 18 **vesper** evening.

 28 **broideries** embroideries.

 33 **Aaron's breastplate** among the images Bertha sees in the manuscript is this. The reference is to Exodus 28:30: 'And Aaron shall bear the judgment of the children of Israel upon his heart before the Lord continually'.

33–4 **the seven/Candlesticks John saw in Heaven** Revelations 1:20: 'The mystery of the seven stars which thou sawest in my right hand, and the seven golden candlesticks. The seven stars are the angels of the seven churches: and the seven candlesticks which thou sawest are the seven churches'.

 36 **Covenantal Ark** the image of the sacred golden chest containing the two stone tablets given to Moses by God (I Samuel 6: 2–4).

 53 **pleated lawn-frill** a ruff.

 61 **daws** jackdaws.

 77 **winter screen** to exclude draughts.

79–82 A list of the odd creatures on Bertha's screen.

 79 **Lima mice** Madagascan monkeys with pointed faces.

 81 **Macaw** parrot.

     Av'davat the avadavat, an Indian songbird. They were so named because they were exported from the Indian city of Ahmadabad.

93 **eremite**   Christian hermit.
98 **parcelled out**   divided.
99–114 Keats presents Bertha's text in an invented medieval language.
99 **swevenis**   dreams.
105 **modre**   mother.
107 **croce**   cross.
112 **Somdel**   something.
119 **at Venice**   where St Mark is buried.

Bright Star

The final version of *Bright Star* was completed by the middle of April, 1819. The new passionate images in its closing lines are said to have been written for Fanny Brawne, the woman to whom Keats was engaged.

1 **steadfast**   the poet expresses his ideal: to be as constant and faithful as a star.
2 **aloft**   the star is above the earth, and therefore isolated in its splendour, an image that contrasts with the flux of the human condition.
3 **lids**   eyelids, as the star's isolation is further compounded in its state of watching and lack of participation.
4 **Eremite**   a simile, likening the star to a hermit in the service of God. The fact that neither ever sleeps suggests that each is more than human, and therefore impossible to aspire to.
5 **priestlike task**   the rise and fall of the tides are purifying the earth in the same way as the priest purifies the soul.
6 **pure ablution**   ritualistic cleansing.
7–8 The alliteration of the 'm' sounds emphasizes the beauty found on earth, from which the star is cut off.
9 **still**   two meanings: (1) always, and (2) motionless.
10–11 The word *ripening* and the *swell and fall* of his beloved's breast has the poet comparing the change and movement of the human condition with the steadfast and unchangeable nature of the star.

12 **sweet unrest** an oxymoron (contradiction in terms), highlighting the desirable nature of change.

13 **Still, still** the repetition emphasizes the paradox of desiring permanence in a world that is eternal, being driven by time. **tender-taken breath** despite life being transitory, the poet relishes it.

14 **ever** as in lines 11 and 12, stresses that love can last forever. **or else swoon to death** in a sudden change of thought and tone, the poet contemplates dying as a result of the pleasure that comes from love. Both *swoon* and *death* carry sexual connotations, the latter coming from a myth suggesting that every orgasm decreases a man's life by one minute. The stress pattern places great emphasis upon the final word of the poem, adding weight to its meaning – even if love does not enable a man to live forever, he will die in ecstasy.

On a Dream

This poem came to Keats after a dream he had about Dante's *Divine Comedy: Inferno* (c.1304–1308), a dream which he recounted in a letter to his siblings:

I had passed many days in rather a low state of mind and in the midst of them I dreamt of being in that region of Hell. The dream was one of the most delightful enjoyments I ever had in my life – I floated about the whirling atmosphere as it is described with a beautiful figure to whose lips mine were joined... and in the midst of all this cold and darkness I was warm – even flowery tree tops sprung up and we rested on them sometimes with the lightness of a cloud till the wind blew us away again – I tried a Sonnet upon it – there are fourteen lines but nothing of what I felt in it – o that I could dream it every night.

Friday 16 April 1819

You might like to think how the sonnet form adds to the meaning of this poem as you read it.

1 **Hermes** the messenger of the gods. Keats opens with the classical link between Hermes and the poet's imagination; but, rather than journeying to Greece, the imagination will find itself in Hell.

2 **lullèd Argus** according to ancient mythology Argus, the hundred-eyed giant, was lulled to sleep by Hermes's playing of the lyre before being killed.

3 **Delphic** of Delphi, the main shrine of Apollo, god of the sun, music and poetry.

7 **Ida** a mountain in Greece, where Zeus was raised in a cave.

8 **Tempe** a beautiful valley in the north-east of Thessaly, Greece, renowned for being the haunt of Apollo and the Muses.
Jove Jupiter, the king of the gods, who laid out the plan for Hermes's killing of Argus.

9 **that second circle of sad hell** in the fifth canto of Dante's *Inferno*, Dante and Virgil descend to the second circle, where the souls of the lustful are sent.

10 **flaw** gust.

La Belle Dame sans Merci

In *La Belle Dame sans Merci*, written in April 1819, Keats imitates the folk ballad form. A narrative song, the ballad is usually written in short stanzas, using repetition and a regular stress pattern. Traditionally, the stress pattern is 4, 3, 4, 3; but Keats has a much shorter line (two stresses) to close each of his stanzas. This serves to bring the stanza up short, leaving the reader to note the sense of change.

On a narrative level, stanzas I–III describe an anonymous passer-by questioning the knight, since he looks so weary and haggard. The knight makes his answer in stanzas IV–XII, saying that he has become consumed by love for a beautiful lady. It appears that she has forsaken him, leaving him bereft, and enslaved by his feelings of unspent passion.

Despite this very simple narrative, Keats leaves us with many unanswered questions, in what is regarded as one of his most mysterious poems. By the end, the reader is no clearer as to the meaning of the knight's experience – is his dream real or feigned, and is he suffering from the effects of unrequited love or self-delusion?

La Belle Dame sans Merci translates as 'the beautiful woman without mercy'. As you analyse the poem, is there any evidence to suggest that the lady is deliberately cruel to the knight?

1 **knight-at-arms** a fully-armoured soldier from the medieval period, who travels on horseback. This is just one of many words used to evoke a medieval atmosphere. Can you find some others?

3 **the sedge has withered** marsh grass that has withered, like the knight, echoing the link between the knight and nature.

6 **woe-begone** full of sorrow and sadness. Note that lines 1/2 and 5/6 use repetition with a slight variation; this is called 'incremental repetition', and is a well-known device of the folk ballad.

8 **the harvest's done** connecting the spent knight with nature, there is the suggestion that a more plentiful and fulfilling life presents itself as an alternative.

9 **lily** a flower that symbolizes both purity and death.

10 **anguish moist and fever-dew** a hint of something unnatural, linked to the knight's misery.

12 **withereth** the repetition of the notion of decay and decline.

13 **meads** meadows.

14 **a faery's child** a spirit, and therefore unnatural.

18 **fragrant zone** a perfumed girdle.

19 **as** as if.

26 **manna-dew** while the Israelites wandered through the wilderness, God sent them a dew which gained substance, turning into a food (manna).

27 **language strange** this suggests that the lady is enchanted, and therefore unnatural; their language is not the same.

29 **elfin grot** pretty grotto. As the knight resides with the lady there, he does not realize that he cannot continue to stay in this enchanted land of the imagination.

38 **death-pale** the lady's former lovers in the knight's dream are

all men of power – kings, princes and warriors – and their paleness is symbolic of death.

40 **in thrall** enthralled, enslaved. Perhaps the knight is self-deluded, having ignored all the warning signs telling him of the lady's *wild* nature; nonetheless, the destructive nature of love is a common theme in the folk ballad.

41 **starved lips in the gloam** in the perishing twilight hours, the lady's past lovers were not nourished by her love, but rather starved.

45 **sojourn** stay.

46–8 The repetition of the language in the opening and final stanzas suggests little movement, and that the knight has come full circle. The irony is that, despite no real sense of physical movement, the knight has been ravaged emotionally. Perhaps, in reaching for the ideal, he has been destroyed by something that he cannot have in the real world.

Ode to Psyche

The first of a group of odes written in April 1819, this poem was first published in 1822. In a letter to his brother and sister, dated 30 April 1819, Keats insisted that *Ode to Psyche* 'is the first and only [poem] with which I have taken even moderate pains... This I have done leisurely – I think it reads the more richly for it and will I hope encourage me to write other thing[s] in even a more peaceable and healthy spirit.'

The poem is an allegory, as Psyche is a symbol for the soul (or mind), seen often as, specifically, the imagination, as she crosses the line between mortality and immortality. It is sometimes thought significant that Fanny Brawne, to whom Keats was to become engaged, had moved to Wentworth Place, next door, at the time that this poem was written. Having love as his main theme, and writing that only constant love can achieve immortality, Keats opens with kisses and ends with love personified.

1 **O Goddess!**   these words introduce a long invocation, beginning with a speech (apostrophe) to an unnamed goddess. Does it matter whether the poet saw Psyche, or whether he merely imagined the meeting?
   tuneless numbers   the verses (*numbers*) are unmelodic, as the poet is lacking the necessary inspiration.

4 **soft-conchèd**   shaped like a soft shell.

6 **winged Psyche**   in Greek, *Psyche* translates as both 'soul' and 'butterfly'. As the butterfly flies from its chrysalis, so the soul flies from the body. Cupid also has wings.

7 **thoughtlessly**   in a mood full of abstract thoughts.

13 The use of hyphenated double epithets in this and the following lines evokes vivid images.

14 **Tyrian**   purple, from the dye of Ancient Tyria.

15 **bedded grass**   the creatures make the grass their bed.

16 **pinions**   wings.

20 **aurorean**   related to Aurora, the Roman goddess of the dawn.

21 **wingèd boy**   Cupid, the Roman god of love.

23 **Psyche**   the goddess to whom the poet wishes all of his worship to be directed. Consider the descriptive images used to delineate Cupid and Psyche.

24–39 The poet focuses upon the failure of the ancients to worship Psyche.

25 **Olympus' faded hierarchy**   Mount Olympus was said to be the home of the ancient Greek gods and goddesses. By the time that Psyche had been named among them, Christianity was making its mark.

26 **Phoebe's sapphire-regioned star**   the moon, since Phoebe was the moon goddess.

27 **Vesper**   the planet Venus, or the evening star, associated with the Roman goddess of love; hence the description *amorous*.

30 **virgin-choir**   as in a Greek ritual.
   delicious moan   beautiful lamentation of grief (a contradiction in terms, or oxymoron).

33 **censer**   a container for burning incense, often swung at religious ceremonies.

36–49 There is a focus upon music in this stanza, which is constructed as a sonnet.

36 **antique vows** vows of antiquity.

37 **fond believing lyre** the pagan priests performing music in religious worship, as well as the poet, who in traditional imagery composes verse at the lyre.

38 **haunted forest boughs** in classical myths, nymphs lived in the forests.

41 **lucent fans** translucent or shining wings.

42 **faint** fading.

50 **Yes, I will be** the poet's verbs in this final stanza are in the future tense, perhaps suggesting a commitment to the future, if only in the poet's imagination. Why is the poet's invocation of Psyche a solitary endeavour?
fane temple.

51 **untrodden region** where no one of his own age can reach him.

52 **pleasant pain** an oxymoron, as the poet's thoughts travel in every direction.

55 **Fledge** adorn with feathers.

56 **zephyrs** soft or gentle breezes.

57 **Dryads** wood nymphs.

59 **sanctuary** a holy place. Why does Keats use religious imagery in this final stanza?

60 **wreathed trellis of a working brain** an image that yokes nature with the imagination. The image of the brain working contrasts with lines 1–7, before he met Psyche and gained inspiration from her.

62 **Fancy** the fancy, or imagination, personified as a gardener improving nature. See Keats's poem *Fancy*.

65 **shadowy** perhaps suggesting disillusionment.

66 **casement** window.

Ode to a Nightingale

This ode was written in early May 1819, and Keats's friend Charles Brown recorded the events of its conception:

In the spring of 1819 a nightingale had built her nest near my house. Keats felt a tranquil and continual joy in her song; and one morning he took his chair from the breakfast-table to the grass-plot under a plum-tree, where he sat for two or three hours. When he came into the house, I perceived he had some scraps of paper in his hand, and these he was quietly thrusting behind the books. On enquiry, I found those scraps, four or five in number, contained his poetic feeling on the song of our nightingale. The writing was not well legible; and it was difficult to arrange the stanzas on so many scraps. With his assistance I succeeded, and this was his *Ode to a Nightingale*, a poem which has been the delight of everyone.

H. E. Rollins, *The Keats Circle*, ii 65

Although the ode is regular in both rhyme and rhythm – as a conventional ode should be – there is no pattern to the thoughts that the poet expresses with freedom throughout.

2 **hemlock** a poisonous plant.

3 **opiate** poppy-juice, used to induce sleep.

4 **Lethe-wards** towards the river of forgetfulness, Lethe in Hades.

7 **Dryad** a wood nymph that lives in a tree; the nymph is said to die at the same precise moment as the tree.

11 **vintage** wine. What state of feeling does the poet seem to associate with wine? Bear in mind that he wants to achieve some of the qualities that the nightingale possesses.

13 **Flora** goddess of flowers and fertility.

14 **Provençal song** a song from Provence, in southern France, a place associated with pleasure.

16 **Hippocrene** a spring sacred to the Muses. Drinking its water was said to inspire poets.

17 **beaded bubbles winking at the brim** the alliteration in this image helps to capture the action of the sparkling alcohol. Look for other examples of alliteration in this poem.

21 **Fade** this word is repeated from the last line of stanza 2. This is in order to pull the two stanzas together, and blend the poet's thoughts seamlessly.

26 This line is perhaps an allusion to the early death of Keats's brother, Tom, who died on 1 December 1818, of tuberculosis.

28 **leaden-eyed despairs** lead is a heavy metal, and this reference suggests that life for the poet is intolerable.

32 **Bacchus and his pards** Roman god of wine, whose chariot was drawn by leopards.

33 **viewless** invisible.
   Poesy poetry.

34 How might it be argued that the *dull brain perplexes and retards?*

37 **Fays** fairies.

38 Having appeared to join the bird, this stanza continues in darkness. How would you characterize such a lack of light, in the context of the poet's feelings?

40 **verdurous** full of green vegetation.

41 In darkness, the poet has to rely upon his other senses. What senses does he depend upon?

43 **embalmèd** can mean (1) preserved as are the dead, (2) treasured like memories, or (3) fragrant. Keats is literally referring to the latter meaning, but may be alluding to the others.

46 **eglantine** honeysuckle.

51 **Darkling** in the darkness.

52 **easeful Death** the poet has yearned to die for a long time, imagining death to be pain-free and as blissful as the nightingale's song. Note that the bird is said to sing with *full-throated ease* (10) earlier in the poem.

60 **requiem** a musical performance as a memorial to the dead. After the poet's death, the bird will go on singing.

61 **immortal Bird!** contrasting his own mortality with the immortality of the nightingale, the poet could well be suggesting the link between the bird's song and his own poetry. What else do you think the nightingale symbolizes?

62 **hungry generations** an image suggesting the selfish and empty lives of human beings throughout time.

66 **Ruth** in the book of the Old Testament named after her, Ruth goes into exile and suffers poverty. Read the story of Ruth in the Old Testament. How is Keats's allusion to her significant?

69 **casements** windows.

70 **faery lands forlorn** a reference to the nightingale's song being heard throughout time in fairytales. Note that the tone is negative, associating an enchanting world with pain and sadness. What other images in this stanza do the same?

73 **fancy**   imagination.
75 **plaintive anthem**   a hymn of sadness.
77 **buried deep**   both a literal reference to the distance between the poet and the bird, and an image of death.
79–80 The final two lines are framed as questions. What is the poet questioning?

Ode on a Grecian Urn

This ode was written in May 1819, and depicts the poet's reaction to a decorated Grecian urn that he has pictured in his mind. The form is the same as *Ode to a Nightingale*, but this time the sense evoked is that of sight rather than hearing. Here, Keats philosophizes upon the notion that art – which is artificial and not natural, like the nightingale – provides the only beauty that survives.

1 **still**   can be read as both an adjective (unmoving) and an adverb (until now).
3 **Sylvan historian**   the urn is addressed (apostrophized) as a woodland storyteller, that is narrating with images. This story is offered to us through a series of questions.
5 **leaf-fringed**   the decoration on the urn.
7 **Tempe**   a beautiful Greek valley.
Arcady   Arcadia was thought to be an earthly heaven, the home to Pan and other shepherds.
8 **loth**   reluctant to yield.
10 **timbrels**   tambourines or small drums.
10–14 note the repetition of *pipe(s)* and *ear* (the latter also relating to 'h*ear*d', 'un*hear*d' and 'end*ear*ed'), which lends a hypnotic feel to the verse. The same sort of repetition is presented syntactically in stanzas 2 and 3, where Keats presents his thoughts in a series of apostrophes followed by either assertions (*ever*) or negations (*never, no, not*).
11–12 The imagination can produce sweeter music than real melodies.
14 **ditties of no tone**   songs that cannot be heard.

30 The love that the youth and the maiden enjoy is far better than human love, which is transient, leaving only pain and satiety.

37 **emptied of this folk** the deserted town is symbolic of Keats's vision and fear of death.

this pious morn note that the tense is the present, suggesting that art lives here. The experience of art gives pleasure before – as in reality – pleasure becomes displeasure.

39 **silent** the silent streets suggest no more music – which, in turn, suggests the poet's inability to express answers to his own questions. Ultimately, the urn is about aesthetic experience and sensation.

41 **Attic** of ancient Athens.

brede embroidery.

44–5 **dost tease us out of thought/As doth eternity** both the beauty of the urn and the notion of eternity are to be felt, and not speculated upon. Art stops time, and so is a form of eternity.

45 **Pastoral** the idealized rural life of the Arcadian shepherd (relating back to line 7).

49 **Beauty is truth, truth beauty** this is probably the most controversial of all Keats's lines. It has been suggested that Keats is seeing an everlasting truth in the artificial beauty of the urn; the representational stories depicted there can never change, lending its images a sort of permanence. The imagination fires this eternal beauty and happiness, whereby art is dependent on the senses; and this creates an emotional state that will go on to speak to succeeding generations.

Ode on Melancholy

This ode was written in May/June, 1819. Having read Robert Burton's *Anatomy of Melancholy*, Keats agrees with Burton's theory that the melancholic ought to embrace pain as well as other human feelings and emotions.

The abrupt opening to this ode may well have something to do with the fact that the first stanza was originally the second.

This is the original opening stanza:

> Though you should build a bark of dead men's bones,
>   And rear a phantom gibbet for a mast,
> Stitch creeds together for a sail, with groans
>   To fill it out, blood-stained and aghast;
> Although your rudder be a dragon's tail
>   Long severed, yet still hard with agony,
>   Your cordage large uprootings from the skull
> Of bald Medusa, certes you would fail
>   To find the Melancholy – whether she
>   Dreameth in any isle of Lethe dull.

Why do you think that Keats rejected this opening? Which do you prefer?

1 **No** the first stanza is full of negative words, with the opening line containing four of them. Note the rhythm of line 1, where the stressed beats fall upon the negatives.
   Lethe one of the rivers in the Underworld (Hades), which induced forgetfulness.
2 **Wolf's-bane** a poisonous plant, with yellow flowers.
4 **nightshade** another poisonous plant.
   Proserpine the daughter of Demeter, goddess of fertility, in ancient Greek mythology. She was kidnapped by Pluto, who took her down to Hades, the realm over which he ruled. Demeter grievingly searched for her, and the earth became barren and infertile. Pluto agreed to release Proserpine, but one of her final acts – the eating of a pomegranate from Hades – committed her to return there for six months of every year. This story accounts for the changing of the seasons, as Proserpine's return to the mortal world each year brings spring and summer.
5 **rosary** prayer beads.
   yew-berries poisonous berries of the yew, a tree associated with death and graveyards.
6 **beetle** death-watch beetle. The Egyptians saw the beetle as a sacred creature, and the scarab variety was placed in tombs to secure resurrection.

death-moth   moth with skull-like markings.

7 **Psyche**   in Greek, the soul or the mind, as well as the butterfly (see *Ode to Psyche*, note to line 6, page 172).
  owl   associated with death, due to its nocturnal habits and mournful-sounding cries.

8 **mysteries**   secret rites.

9 **shade**   ghost.

10 **drown the wakeful anguish**   deaden the conscious suffering.

11 **fit**   a sudden, inescapable and unpredictable attack.

11–14 there is a sense of irony in these lines: the rain makes the flowers droop, but also *fosters* them to grow; there is a death image in *shroud*, but the month is April – and the outlook is positive; the hill is hidden by the rain, but the hill is *green*, and the lack of vision is temporary.

12 **heaven**   the source of melancholy is the rain, but the reference to heaven may well be linked to the idea of melancholy as a goddess.

14 **shroud**   a piece of cloth used to cover a dead body.

15 **glut**   feed or gorge upon.

15–20 These lines suggest nature's antidotes for melancholy: the *morning rose* is fragile, and will not last long; the *rainbow* and the *salt sand-wave* are transitory, but will return; the *peonies* are shrubs that will lose their colourful flowers in time; and, though a victim of his *mistress's* fury, the lover can still find appreciation in her beauty. What is Keats's theory about the transience of life?

21 **She**   both melancholy and the beloved.

23 **bidding adieu**   as we appreciate beauty and joy, they are already disappearing.
  aching Pleasure   an oxymoron, perhaps suggesting a sexual element.

24–26 Nature imagery consolidates the point. Melancholy has her shrine in the *temple of Delight*: the two are inseparable and are, here, each presented as a goddess. The point is that melancholy is *veiled* – we cannot see it while experiencing other delights.

28 **palate fine**   only individuals with refined tastes are able to see melancholy in delight. Here, Keats is referring to the aesthetic.

30 **cloudy trophies**   a metaphor for the triumphing mood. The fact that the trophy is cloudy may appear to be negative, but it

may only reinforce the philosophy that pleasure and melancholy are an inescapable mixture. In a letter to his siblings, Keats wrote, 'This is the world – thus we cannot expect to give way many hours to pleasure – Circumstances are like Clouds continually gathering and bursting' (Friday, 19 March 1819). Perhaps Keats is suggesting that it is better to immerse ourselves fully in life, in order to become sensitive (and not deadened) to every feeling.

Ode on Indolence

This ode was probably written in the spring of 1819, although it was not published until after Keats's death. In this poem, indolence is a way of forgetting the pain and frustration caused by the changes and impermanence of reality. Despite the attraction of poetry, indolence cannot abide even this – as poetry requires the poet to feel and think too acutely.

1 **three figures** in the third stanza, these will be named as Love, Ambition and Poetry, sculptural allegorical figures that pose in Greek disguise. For now, they remain *strange* (9) to the poet.

10 **Phidian** relating to Phidias, the Greek sculptor who died in about 432 BC; he is said to have sculpted the frieze of the Parthenon. The poet argues that he is an academic, but has not the expertise of Phidian lore.

11 **How is it, Shadows!** the poet addresses the figures directly. He seems not to have recognized his own soul, with Ambition as the motive for Poesy, and Love as the subject.

12 **hush a masque** quietly disguised.

13 **silent deep-distinguishèd plot** the poet now considers the figures to have a quiet but cunning plan for him.

11–20 Despite the inactivity that is a product of indolence in this stanza, why do you think that the drowsy hour is *Ripe*, the cloud is *blissful*, his pulse is growing in its lessening, the wreath is *pleasure's*, and indolence itself belongs to *summer*?

15–20 The poet's first consideration of indolence considers it in terms of insensibility, numbness and death. The repeated *no* (18) and the word *nothingness* serve to emphasize his idle days and *benumbed* vision.

30 **demon Poesy** poetry, which he is compelled to write.

31 **I wanted wings** the poet displays irony as, when the spirits fade, he wishes to follow them.

37 **honeyed indolence** the untroubled state that the poet hankers after.

39 **how change the moons** a reference to the speed of time, which dictates life and reminds the poet of his own mortality.

42 **dim dreams** the poet now considers indolence as a state, not of unconsciousness, but of rich thoughts and dreams.

48 **throstle's lay** the thrush's song.

51 **So, ye three Ghosts, adieu!** once again, the poet invokes the spirits directly. The poet admits that the spirits were right to leave, for they have failed to raise him. How is this assertion ironic?

54 Keats argues that love is sentiment, and that a sentimental constitution is one to be mocked. Ironically, he wishes not to feel the very things that will go on to make him a great poet.

57/8 **visions** the repetition of this word suggests that the poet does recognize sensation, albeit vaguely.

59 **Phantoms** do you think it is significant that the three figures are seen initially as *shades* (8), then *Shadows* (11), *Ghosts* (51) and finally *Phantoms* (59)?

Lamia

Written between May and September 1819, this narrative poem is structured in heroic couplets after the fashion of John Dryden, with an iambic pentameter rhythm (ten syllables, mainly consisting of an unstressed followed by a stressed syllable). Occasionally, Keats presents his reader with a triplet and an alexandrine (a line with two extra syllables) to vary the pace.

A lamia was traditionally a female monster with a serpent's body and a woman's head and breasts. Although she could not speak, she was able to hiss – and such hissing was said to attract passing strangers, whom she would then eat.

In Greek mythology, Lamia was the beautiful queen of Libya, daughter of Belus and Libya. Zeus fell in love with her, but a jealous Hera found out about the affair and killed all the children that Lamia had borne. Lamia was so grief-stricken that she entered a cave and unleashed her anger by killing pregnant women in order to devour the foetuses inside; she was also said to suck the blood of captured human children. In one version of the myth, Lamia's child-killing activities deformed her body over time; in another version, it was Hera herself who deliberately deformed her husband's lover at the outset.

According to Jewish folklore, the lamia is associated with Adam's first wife, Lilith. She was said to have been created by God out of the earth, as was Adam himself. However, she refused to be a good mate to Adam, arguing against subservience: 'We are equal to each other inasmuch as we were both created from the earth'. Lilith then shouted out God's name, and flew into the air and away from Paradise. God sent three angels – Snvi, Snsvi and Smnglof – to try to convince Lilith to return, but to no avail. God cursed her, by sentencing one hundred of her children to die each day; and it was decreed that only by placing the names of the three angels over a woman's bed could she be protected during childbirth.

Philostratus's *Life of Apollonius* tells of the lamiae. One of Apollonius's students, Menippus, fell in love with the apparition of a beautiful woman. The apparition told him where to find her, and Menippus told Apollonius about the situation. Unfortunately, Apollonius had the worst possible news for his student: 'This fine bride is one of the... lamiae... These beings fall in love, and they are devoted to the delights of Aphrodite, but especially in the flesh of human beings, and they decoy with such delights those whom they mean to devour in their feasts'. When confronted, the beautiful woman admitted to her true identity, and to cravings for the pure and strong blood of the very young.

Robert Burton, in his *Anatomy of Melancholy* (1621), took Philostratus's story and further elaborated upon it:

Philostratus in his fourth book *de vita Apollonii*, hath a memorable instance... of one Menippus Lycius, a young man twenty-five years of age, that going between Cenchreas and Corinth, met such a phantasm in the habit of a fair gentlewoman, which, taking him by the hand, carried him home to her house in the suburbs of Corinth, and told him she was a Phoenician by birth, and if he would tarry with her, 'he should hear her sing and play, and drink such wine as never any drank, and no man should molest him; but she being fair and lovely would live and die with him, that was fair and lovely to behold.' The young man, a philosopher, otherwise staid and discreet, able to moderate his passions, though not this of love, tarried with her awhile to his great content, and at last married her, to whose wedding, amongst other guests, came Apollonius, who, by some probable conjectures, found her out to be a serpent, a lamia, and that all her furniture was like Tantalus's gold described by Homer, no substance, but mere illusions. When she saw herself descried, she wept, and desired Apollonius to be silent, but he would not be moved, and thereupon she, plate, house, and all that was in it, vanished in an instant: 'many thousands took notice of this fact, for it was done in the midst of Greece.'

Part 3, Section 2, pp.46–47

This is clearly Keats's source for the poem.

Part I

 2 **Satyr**   half-man, half-goat.
 3 **King Oberon**   king of the fairies in Shakespeare's *A Midsummer Night's Dream*.
 5 **the Dryads and the Fauns**   wood nymphs and satyr-like creatures.
 7 **Hermes**   messenger of the gods, famous for his love affairs.
 9 **Olympus**   according to legend, the Greek mountain that was home to the gods.
11 **summoner**   Jove.
15 **Tritons**   sea gods, said to be human above the waist and dolphin below.

18 **meads** meadows.

30 This line is an alexandrine (having two extra syllables) in order to vary the pace.

46 **cirque-couchant** coiled in a circle.

47 **gordian** a complicated knot; this relates to Greek legend and King Gordias of Phrygia, who tied a knot that Alexander the Great cut through with his sword.

49 **pard** leopard.

55 **penanced lady elf** suggests that being trapped inside the body of a serpent is Lamia's punishment for some past deed.

56 **demon's mistress** devil's lover.

57 **wannish** pale.

58 **Ariadne's tiar** a constellation of stars.

63 **Proserpine** in ancient Greek mythology, a goddess who was captured by Pluto and taken by force to the Underworld. See note to line 4 of *Ode on Melancholy*, page 178.

65 **bubbling honey** love is associated with excess; this notion links back to line 59 and the oxymoron *bitter-sweet*.

66 **pinions** wings.

74 **Apollo** the Greek god of poetry and music, often identified with the sun.

78 **Phoebean dart** a sunbeam; this comes from the notion of Phoebus (the Roman equivalent of Apollo) shooting his arrow.

81 **star of Lethe** Hermes, the messenger god, who took the dead across the Underworld's river Lethe.

84 **beauteous wreath** a symbol that suggests the serpent is the minister of death.

89 **serpent rod** Hermes's wand, which was entwined by two snakes.

100 Goddess-like, Lamia protects the nymph.

103 **Silenus** an old satyr, well-known for his drinking and lechery.

106 **steep** soak.

107 **syrops** syrups; magic potions.

111 **boon** favour or request.

114 **psalterian** like the music from a psalter, a stringed instrument.

115 **Circean** like Circe, the Greek enchantress, famed for her magic arts and potions.

116 **damask** red.

117–8 These lines hint at Lamia's past, and the fact that she was a mortal once before.

119 **a youth of Corinth** Lycius.

124 **breathed** suggests God's breathing of life into Adam.

131 **verdure** greenery.

133 **Caducean charm** the spell administered by the caduceus, Hermes's wand.

143 **lees** dregs.

148 **besprent** sprinkled.

151 **sear** dried up.

158 **brede** an archaic spelling of 'braid'.

163 **rubious-argent** reddish silver.

174 **Cenchreas** a town on the isthmus of Corinth, in Greece.

176 **Peraean rills** mountain springs.

179 **Cleone** a village between Argos and Corinth.

188 The image is of dancing to music, with a green skirt splaying.

189–90 A virgin who knows as much about love as the most experienced of lovers.

191 **sciential** possessing knowledge (of love, in this case).

192 **unperplex** disentangle.

195 **dispart** separate.

198 **unshent** innocent.

204 **list** wished for.

206 **Elysium** according to Greek legend, the place where human souls enjoy perfect happiness.

207 **Nereids** sea nymphs, being daughters of Nereus.

208 **Thetis** mother of Achilles, and a sea goddess.

209 **Bacchus** the Roman god of wine.

211 **Pluto** the Greek god of the Underworld.
palatine palatial.

212 **Mulciber** John Milton's name for Vulcan, the Roman god of fire and metalworking.
piazzian line a continuous line of columns surrounding a piazza.

225 **Egina isle** an island in the Aegean Sea.

236 **Platonic shades** thoughts of Plato, the fourth-century BC Greek philosopher.

244 **syllabling** saying.

248 **Orpheus-like at an Eurydice** Orpheus was told that his lover, Eurydice, could be saved from the Underworld if he led her to earth without looking back at her once. Failing to do this, Orpheus lost his love forever.

261 **Naiad** water nymph.

265 **Pleiad** according to myth, she was one of the sisters turned into stars by Zeus.

283 **essence** the material that gods are made of.

285 **sleights** tricks.

293 **slow amenity** gradually becoming more agreeable.

320 **the Adonian feast** the celebration dedicated to Adonis, lover of Venus.

329 **Peris** good fairies.

332 **lineal** descended.

333 **Pyrrha's pebbles** this legend goes back to Ovid's *Metamorphoses*. After a great flood, Deucalion and Pyrrha dropped stones behind them, which metamorphosed into humans, thus repopulating the earth.

347 **blinded Lycius** he is so infatuated with Lamia, Lycius does not notice that she has cast a spell in order that they reach Corinth more quickly.

375 **Apollonius sage** the wise magician and philosopher, Apollonius. Note the inverted word order for emphasis.

386 **Aeolian** like a wind harp.

394 **flitter-wingèd** light-winged, and thus able to fly anywhere.

Part II

6 **non-elect** those who have not loved.

9 **clenched** clinched.

24 **tithe** a tenth, a small amount.

30 **harboured** sheltered.

33 **forsworn** rejected or renounced.

34 **penetrant** sharp, penetrating.

36 **empery** empire.

39 **passion's passing-bell** the death of passion; reminiscent of *Ode to a Nightingale: the very word is like a bell*, line 71.

76 **sanguineous** full of blood.

79–80 According to Greek legend, Python was a dragon that guarded the oracle of Themis in Delphi; it killed any living being that came in its way, and generally polluted and ravaged the earth. Apollo freed the land of this terror by killing Python with his arrows, thus consecrating the shrine.

80 **Certes**   certainly.

97 **rite**   ritual (for the dead).

105 **Of deep sleep**   in order to prevent Lycius questioning her, Lamia puts him in to a deep sleep using her magic.

116 **misery**   Lamia's true self is miserable, fearful of being discovered. Note the alliteration in this line, contrasting what she really is with her disguised *magnificence*.

118 **servitors**   servants.

124 **charm**   spell.

126 **plantain**   a large tropical plant.

136 **Missioned**   ordered, sent on a mission.

137 **fretted**   carefully worked.

146 **rout**   crowd.

151 **amain**   vehemently.

160 **daffed**   opposed.

171 **mien**   look, demeanour.

172 Literally, the wise man's ill-humour is being sweetened. The sibilance in this line echoes the hissing of a serpent – and Lamia's fear of Apollonius.

176 **censer**   a vessel for burning incense.

179 **Wool-woofèd**   woven of wool.

185 **libbard**   leopard.

187 **Ceres' horn**   Ceres is the Roman goddess, corresponding to the Greek Demeter. As the goddess of corn, her fertility symbol is the horn of plenty.

188 **tun**   barrel.

194 **meet**   fitting.

204 Note that the shift to the present tense makes the narrative appear more dramatic and immediate.

207 **nectarous cheer**   intoxicating drinks.

210 **trammels**   restraints, hindrances.

213 **Bacchus**   the Roman god of wine.
   meridian height   the height of the day (noon), suggesting that much wine has been consumed.

217 **osiered**   woven.

224 **willow**   the tree associated with grief; the image suggests weeping.

adder's tongue   a plant with leaves in the shape of a snake's tongue.

226 **thyrsus**   Bacchus's staff.

229–30 The philosophy here is that magic can no longer work if the power of reason is exercised.

231 **awful**   awe-inspiring.

232 **woof**   weave.

234 Again, the argument is that reason negates the wonders and mysteries of life.

236 **gnomèd**   worked by gnomes.

264 **myrtle**   the tree said to be sacred to Venus, the Roman goddess of love. Venus is the Roman equivalent of Aphrodite – but Venus's earliest associations were with fields and gardens, as well as love and female beauty.

268 Every man's hair stood on end with fear.

285 **impious proud-heart sophistries**   irreligious, arrogant reasoning.

291 **sophist**   referring to Apollonius as a teacher of reason and knowledge.

301 **perceant**   piercing.

To Autumn

Written at Winchester on 19 September 1819, this poem was first published in 1820. Keats composed the ode shortly after a Sunday walk in Winchester, and, in a letter to John Hamilton Reynolds dated Tuesday 21 September 1819, Keats described what he felt and saw: 'How beautiful the season is now – How fine the air. A temperate sharpness about it'.

One of Keats's final poems, *To Autumn* describes the season in its early stages of high activity. The first stanza is concerned with the sights of autumn, the second the activities, and the third the sounds. An evocative poem, *To Autumn* is usually described as an ode, as its basic style and structure emulate the odes written in the spring of 1819. Indeed, Harold Bloom suggests that it is 'one of the subtlest and most beautiful of all Keats's odes'. However, Keats does not specify the genre in the poem's title. Why is that, do you think?

The opening stanza is constructed as one sentence, clearly to present it as a whole. Note the absence of a main verb, which throws the emphasis upon the visual images and descriptions of autumn, being a season of ripening and fruition.

   2 **bosom-friend** autumn is personified in an immediate invocation.
      maturing engendering maturity; the sun ripens fruit in a season of plenty.
   6 **ripeness** sweetness.
   7 **gourd** large fleshy fruit.
   8 **kernel** inner seed of a nut or fruit stone.
 8–9 The reference to *budding* suggests fruition, which is ongoing (*still more*).
  11 **clammy cells** the moisture from honeycomb in the beehive. Why do you think that summer is personified in this stanza?
  14 **Thee** autumn is personified as a harvester.
      granary a storehouse for grain.
  15 **winnowing** separating grain from chaff by means of a current of air.
  17 **Drowsed** Autumn is made sleepy by the opium-infused poppies, which grow in fields of grain.
  18 **swath** the strip of corn to be cut by the sweep of the scythe's blade.
  19 **gleaner** a person who gathers the useful remnants of a crop that the reapers have left behind.
  21 **cider-press** a machine that squeezes apples to produce cider.
  22 How does the final line work as a metaphor, and why does Keats use the secondary device of onomatopoeia?
  23 **Spring** the formative time of rebirth, personified to contrast with autumn.
  25 **barrèd clouds** horizontal clouds, resembling bars.
25–6 An image to reinforce the idea of the dying of the day which, while described positively, introduces a feeling of sadness.

26 **stubble**   the stubs of stalks left after harvesting. In his letter to Reynolds, Keats wrote, 'I never lik'd stubble fields so much as now – Aye better than the chilly green of the spring. Somehow a stubble plain looks warm'.

28 **sallows**   willow trees.

30 **full-grown lambs**   those that were born in spring, marking the passing of time.

   hilly bourn   hills demarcating the horizon's boundary.

32 **croft**   a small, enclosed field. How might the end of this stanza be said to represent the close of a day, and the cyclical pattern of nature and of life?

The Fall of Hyperion: A Dream

The Fall of Hyperion, from which this is an extract, was written in September 1819, and was a revised version of the original *Hyperion*. Published posthumously, in 1857, it is an unfinished piece, since Keats believed it to be overly Miltonic in structure. He considered this to be an 'artful' style of writing, rather than 'the true voice of feeling'.

The narrative itself has been likened to Dante's *Divine Comedy*, with its canto structure and the guided journey through Hell, Purgatory and Paradise. The opening lines are in praise of poetry and the dreams that are born of this art.

1 **Fanatics**   religious fanatics.

3 **the loftiest fashion of his sleep**   the dreams of deepest sleep.

7 **laurel**   poetry.

10 **sable charm**   a spell related to death; lines 8–11 suggest that the imagination, held under this death-like spell, can only be released by the power of poetry.

13 **clod**   a hard lump.

27 **censers**   receptacles for incense.

35 **fabled horn**   the cornucopia, or horn of plenty.

37 **Proserpine**   according to legend, the daughter of Ceres had to spend half of the year on earth and the other in the Underworld.

42 **transparent juice** nectar, the drink of the gods.
48 **Caliphat** the Caliphs ruled the Muslim world after
    Mohammed died. They were thought to use poison as a
    weapon in political crime. In *The Arabian Nights*, the jealous
    wife of the Caliph used a poisonous drug on one of her rivals.
50 **scarlet conclave** the group of cardinals who elect the pope.
51 **rapt** taken.
56 **Silenus** the aged attendant to Bacchus, famed for his
    drunkenness and lechery.
68 **superannuations** ruins, antiquity.
75 **that place the moth could not corrupt** in Matthew 6:19–20,
    we are told, 'Lay not up for yourselves treasures upon earth,
    where moth and rust doth corrupt, and where thieves break
    through and steal.'
77 **imageries** embroidered designs in cloth.
79 **chafing-dish** another term for censer.
88 **Image** the image is of Saturn (see line 226).
96 **One ministering** Moneta, the priestess of the temple (see line
    226).
103 **Maian** of May.
116 **gummèd** resinous, aromatic leaves used to create incense.
125 **streams** arteries.
135–6 See the biblical narrative of Jacob's dream in Genesis 28:12.
137 **the hornèd shrine** it was believed that in ancient times altars
    were adorned with horns from the animals that had been
    sacrificed there.
144–5 **dated on/Thy doom** postponed your death.
145–6 **purge off... film** help me to understand more clearly.
152 **fane** temple.
155 **sooth** truthful, as in 'soothsayer'.
169 **A fever of thyself** prone to fits of poetic inspiration.
175 **venoms** poisons.
183 **propitious parley** favourable talk.
190 **humanist** humanitarian.
198 **Pendent** hanging.
200 **antipodes** direct opposite.
203 **Pythia** priestess of Apollo at Delphi, who delivered
    prophecies madly and incoherently.
204 **Apollo** son of Jupiter.

205 **thy misty pestilence** Apollo was often associated with disease
and plague.

208 **careless hectorers in proud bad verse** could well refer to
Byron and Wordsworth.

222 **war** the Titans versus the Olympian gods.

226 **Moneta** Mnemosyne, said to be the mother of the muses.

229 **roofèd home** mouth.

244–5 The remembered images are so vivid that they make her swoon.

246 **electral** charged with electricity.

249 **spherèd** heavenly.

257 **pined** wasted.

265 **benignant** kind.

266 **Soft-mitigated** softened.

267 **visionless** the eyes are unable to see the physical world, as
they are concerned only with inner visions.

282 **'Shade of Memory!'** Mnemosyne means 'memory'.

285 **the golden age** of Saturn's reign.

286 **Apollo, thy dear foster child** Jupiter fathered Apollo by
Latona, despite being married to Metona.

288 **Omega** the last; the survivor of the Titans (derived from the
last letter of the Greek alphabet).

294 This line is significant, as it marks the point at which *Hyperion*
begins.

303 **ken** sight, knowledge.

312 **zoning** duration.

317 **Naiad** water-nymph.

319 **margin-sand** foreshore.

323 **nerveless** having no nerves, weak.

326 **ancient mother** Tellus, which means earth. *The Fall of
Hyperion* continues from here; Canto I has 468 lines, and the
poem is abandoned at Canto II, line 61.

Interpretations

Different methods of interpreting Keats's poetry

From the information on pages 1–12 about Keats's life and works, the importance of contexts should have become clear to you. There are many contexts to be considered, including external ones relating to the Romantic period, as well as internal ones, to do with his own home life, personal relationships and health. We will consider the latter first.

Keats's life

We have seen that Keats travelled to some very beautiful parts of the country. Many of his poems consider nature and the landscape, and it is these references that have led critics to speak of Keats's work as sensuous and imagistic. He is not simply a 'nature poet', however, and as with all the Romantics his references to nature act as a stimulus to thought and imagination. Essentially, natural phenomena help Keats to contemplate central human issues. For example, his *Ode to a Nightingale* is about the bird's song, and how it has led him to evaluate life. While the nightingale's song makes him happy, it reminds him of the unhappiness of life – such that he turns to the imagination to escape from it.

Keats's poems touching upon human love are rather ambivalent, and this could be seen as a reflection of his own feelings about women. While it is clear from his letters that he loved Fanny Brawne, he was never completely happy in the relationship. In many of Keats's letters and some of his poems, he complains of the lack of freedom that comes with falling in love. His preoccupation with death in many of the poems – especially the odes – suggests that Keats had his own troubles and frustrations. *La Belle Dame sans Merci* is a beautiful ballad, which many see as Keats's own attack upon the pains of love. Those poems that deal with heroes and heroines achieving immortality through love – such as *Endymion*, *The Eve of St Agnes* and *Ode to Psyche* – may suggest that Keats believed that his own ideal of love could not survive in this world.

Keats had seen the death of both parents, the departure of one brother to America and the death from tuberculosis of the other. In April and May 1819, Keats poured forth a torrent of poetic energy, which produced such works as *Ode to Psyche*, *Ode on Melancholy*, *Ode on a Grecian Urn* and *Ode on Indolence*. All are often said to have been an emotional outpouring at the loss of his brother, Tom, on 1 December 1818, aged only 19.

After giving up medicine, he had no reliable method of supporting himself. His poetry did not bring the financial rewards he had hoped for. He could not marry Fanny Brawne because he was not in a financial position to do so, and his health was in serious decline. Such concerns can be seen to manifest themselves in the rather gloomy and pessimistic images of *Ode on Melancholy* and *The Fall of Hyperion*.

Keats was a non-Christian, and at no time in his poetry does he rely upon a god or an after-life to redeem mortal ills. Indeed, Keats often replaces religion with mythology, presenting superhuman beings to allegorize good and evil.

Activity

In *Hyperion: A Fragment* (1818), how successful do you think Keats is in introducing his theme of loss and suffering through the myths of the Titans and the Olympians?

Discussion

The poem opens *in medias res* (a Latin phrase meaning 'in the middle of things'), with Saturn and the Titans having already been defeated.

Only Hyperion, the sun god, is free from suffering, as he is still in power – and he attempts to rouse the others to retaliate against the enemy. It is not until Book III that Apollo appears to claim his throne; he is about to be made the new generation's god of the sun, music, healing and prophecy by Mnemosyne, the Titan goddess who has defected. Despite the poem being unfinished, it is still evident that Keats's main focus lies upon the pain caused for both sides. As an allegory, this poem may well be suggesting that, for all humans, the pain of loss is inevitable – and that, for a poet, such feelings are experienced all the more keenly.

Keats's times

By the time Keats was thinking about giving up a promising medical career in favour of writing, the Terror in France had come to an end (July 1794) and the English no longer saw the French model as one to follow. Indeed, the revolutions in both France and America caused many English people to fear the sort of violence that had ensued from the political massacres in those two great nations. As the industrial revolution caused more problems for the lower classes than it solved, in both urban and rural areas, morale was regarded as being at an all-time low. Keats, a man of his times, was already framing his visionary ideas in poetry.

It is therefore impossible to consider Romanticism as merely a poetic phenomenon. Rather, it needs to be considered within its socio-political, literary, philosophical and religious contexts.

In terms of the former, during the period that is now termed 'Romantic', there were three main revolutions that have since been said to have laid the foundations for the modern world.

The American War of Independence

Freedom fighters in 13 of the American colonies made a 'Declaration of Independence' in 1776, aiming to break free from Britain. The author of the Declaration was Thomas Jefferson

(1743–1826), whose aim was to secure the people's 'unalienable rights', and freedom for the American revolutionaries. The British government had been charging the Americans ever higher taxes, while they had no representatives in the Westminster Parliament. King George III was furious that the American colonies were trying to escape from British rule, and he sent his 'redcoats' (British soldiers in scarlet uniforms) to America to force them into submission, loyalty and tax payments. Many of these soldiers were press-ganged into service; they did not have any choice in the matter. Often, men were carried off to serve in either the army or the navy without warning.

In spite of the growing power of Parliament at this time, it was the king who symbolized government, so these soldiers' blood, metaphorically speaking, runs down his palace walls, as in William Blake's poem *London*. The British were to recognize American independence only after a seven-year battle, in 1783.

The French Revolution

Under Louis XVI, there was a large population in France – with most living in rural areas. The eighteenth century had also seen the advent of capitalism, as national and international exchange of goods became increasingly possible. As overseas and domestic trade grew, the divide between the rich and the poor became ever greater. City living exposed people to filthy air and water, and the paid work on offer only served to further worsen health and shorten life spans. In July 1789, the fall of the Bastille prison marked the real beginning of the French Revolution. Britain's war with France began in 1793, with the Reign of Terror continuing into the following year. There was a respite after the Treaty of Amiens in 1802, but war was soon to resume and continue into 1815. The economic and human cost of the conflict was immense.

Many writers, philosophers and journalists helped to shape the ideas that would lead to revolution, including Thomas Paine (1737–1809). Born in Thetford, England, Paine moved to

Philadelphia in the US as an adult, and his journalistic writing made him famous; he paved the way for much egalitarian and humanitarian thinking. Known as one of the Founding Fathers, Paine inspired great passion and delivered a grand vision for American society. In particular, his *Common Sense* (1776) and *The Crisis* (1776–1783) describe and condone the beginning of the American Revolution.

Similarly, in France the unconventional Jean-Jacques Rousseau (1712–1778) wrote in order to share his controversial political thoughts. His *Discourse on the Political Economy* (1755) influenced the French Revolution, while his *Discourse on the Origin of Inequality* (1754) argued that every human injustice is a result of the artificial control exercised by intellect and politics over healthy natural impulses. In Rousseau's most celebrated work, *The Social Contract* (1762), he puts forward the notion of a civil society formed by its citizens. At its heart is the philosophy that perfect freedom is the natural condition of all human beings.

Rousseau supported the views of John Locke (1632–1704). Locke's *Two Treatises of Government* (1689) had proposed a social contract theory of government, and argued against a belief in the divine right of kings. Locke believed that a government should be elected in order to safeguard natural rights – what he termed life, liberty and estate. These ideas helped to shape the views of the early revolutionaries.

The agrarian and industrial revolutions

In 1815, when the war with France was over, many British citizens expected improvements in the economy and society. Unfortunately, Britain's problems worsened. Despite an increasing population and poor harvest yields, the new laws on enclosing land meant that employment in farming was hard hit, and the Corn Laws of 1815, which kept the price of corn artificially high, added to inflation and widened still further the gap between rich and poor. The rapid expansion of coal and iron production, as well as the development of the steam engine, meant that industry was growing; but the wealth created all went to the landed gentry, and labour-saving machinery led to a further loss of jobs for the working people.

Meanwhile, cottage industries were growing, where women and children were favoured as workers over a more expensive male, urban workforce. Most workers were expected to work for 12 hours a day without a break in hazardous conditions. Wages were driven down, and the cost of living was going up. With cities providing only the most squalid of accommodation for the poor and needy, life both at home and at work was full of hardships.

The Romantic poets directly address these issues on occasion. For example, in the spring of 1792, Wordsworth wrote Books IX–XI of his *Prelude*, which were inspired by the rapidly changing world. In Book IX, the narrator expresses the belief that war is the only way that justice will be done for the poor and lowly.

Blake's *London* (from *Songs of Experience*, 1793) opens: *I wander through each chartered street,/Near where the chartered Thames does flow*. It is unlikely that Blake intended *chartered* to mean 'free', since the city's charter, while increasing ownership of land for the well-to-do, meant a loss of freedom for the less privileged.

Coleridge believed his work *Fears in Solitude*, written in the April 1798, to be 'perhaps not poetry, but perhaps a sort of middle thing between poetry and oratory'. An anti-war poem, it presents the poet's thoughts regarding the potential invasion of a French army in 1798. This is viewed as an attack not only against the English, but also against God, and perhaps as terrible revenge for prevailing injustices.

Activity

Consider some examples of how Keats might – directly or indirectly – write about socio-political events.

Discussion

Keats was said to belong to the 'Cockney School' of poets, a derogatory term that stuck to him. John Gibson Lockhart, writing in *Blackwood's Edinburgh Magazine*, did the most damage to Keats's reputation – not surprisingly, since the publication was one of the foremost Tory magazines of the day. Placing Leigh Hunt, Shelley, Byron, William Hazlitt and Charles Lamb into the same 'school' meant that many targets could be hit at once. He sneered at Keats's lack of classical education, and implied he lacked sense in having given up a promising career in medicine for a doubtful one in poetry. Such personal attacks were common, and it followed that Keats's poetry would be poorly reviewed.

The writer Leigh Hunt (1784–1859)

Percy Bysshe Shelley, painted in 1819

Recent scholars now consider it likely that Keats's poor reviews in the early days were a result not so much of his poetic style, structure and content, but rather of his associations with those out of favour politically. His experimental techniques were thought to be far too revolutionary – especially in an age of revolution. As a liberal, Keats's early poems can be considered allegories for the political age in which he lived. For example, in *Hyperion: A Fragment*, which narrates the legendary overthrow of the Titans, Keats welcomes in a new generation at the expense of the old. This notion certainly reflects his denunciation of the nobility, and the fact that, in his eyes, '[t]here is of a truth nothing manly or sterling in any part of the Government' (October 1818).

However, despite it being clear that the political climate of the time influenced the subject of the poem, it is also apparent that Keats's political beliefs never dominated his main belief in poetry. Indeed, Richard Cronin argues that, 'On the evidence of the poems it might seem that Keats's recent critics are a good deal more interested in politics than he was himself' ('Leigh Hunt, Keats and the Politics of Cockney Poetry', in *The Politics of Romantic Poetry*). The revolutionary aspects of his age did creep into his poetic expression, but, as time went on, Keats's work developed to embrace the notions of suffering and how mortals might better appreciate their time on earth. This is political in the true sense of the word; a sympathetic Keats shows himself to be in tune with man, nature and the poetic imagination.

Literary and philosophical influences

Features of Romantic poetry

As a Romantic poet, Keats believed in the power of genuine feeling, wanting the individual to set free his or her own mind – or at the very least the imagination – in order to live life more freely. In essence, Romantic poetry was often about the solitary figure engaged on a lone quest to find a higher reality. Keats termed this 'truth', an ethos that the various revolutions of the time had engendered. The American and French revolutions of the previous century had set the stage for freedom and endless possibilities, while the agrarian and industrial revolutions also had a profound effect upon people's lives and aspirations.

Most Romantic poets believed in freedom of self-expression in order to present a personal vision and their own imaginative truths. The power of the imagination – or fancy – is particularly relevant in Keats's *Ode to a Nightingale*, although ultimately in this poem he is forced to admit that *fancy cannot cheat so well/As she is famed to do*. The poem entitled *Fancy* is about just this: allowing the imagination to run free. According to the Romantics, this can only lead to sincerity, spontaneity and originality.

The Romantic poets placed value upon emotional intensity. Keats achieves this throughout his poetry, but his sonnets encapsulate emotion into the smallest of spaces. For example, the sonnet *When I have Fears* is full of rich images of the harvest, which help Keats to focus upon some of his most important issues – ambition, time and death – in only 14 lines.

The Romantics also saw the value of an imaginative interest in the irrational realms of dream and delirium, or folk superstition and legend. Keats's *Eve of St Agnes* is a poem set in a medieval castle, and deals with knights and their ladies, old dames, superstitions and magic. In this poem, Keats's real interest is romantic love, which he idealizes and puts on a level with the supernatural.

Using the benign influence and rhythms of the natural world, the Romantics hoped to stimulate the imagination. In one of Keats's final poems, *To Autumn*, he piles up autumnal imagery in order to create the most sumptuous and sensuous of descriptions. Autumn is personified as a friend, a thresher, a reaper, a gleaner and a cider-maker, in order to best convey the business of the season.

The pursuit of happiness is a key Romantic concern. In Keats's *Ode on a Grecian Urn*, he meditates upon the problem of happiness and its brevity in life. Only art can offer permanence; the urn can offer a truth and a picture of happiness which may, or may not, be offered after death for the observer.

Humanitarianism in Keats's poetry

Wordsworth and Coleridge's *Lyrical Ballads* first stressed the Romantic notion of humanitarianism, with several of the poems concerning themselves with poverty, the problem of vagrancy and the futility of war. Wordsworth's *The Female Vagrant* (derived from *Salisbury Plain*, written in 1793, and revised for inclusion in *Lyrical Ballads* in 1798) is among the most famous. It is about a woman whose husband and offspring are finally killed *by sword/And ravenous plague* (132/3), leaving her an outcast.

Aiden Day, in his book *Romanticism*, adds Coleridge's *The Dungeon* (1797) to the list of what he terms 'humanitarian protests [which] were poetically highly defined and often specially subtle'. He alerts us to Coleridge's horror at 'dehumanising prison conditions' which only served to 'stagnate and corrupt', driving a 'deformed' man to 'sights of ever more deformity'. Keats's poem *Isabella, or The Pot of Basil* (1818) continued the tradition, arguing against the human suffering that is a direct result of capitalism (see stanzas XIV–XVII).

Unrest among the working people frightened the Tory government of the day, and many expected a revolution. Any radical was punished severely under the most stringent laws, while propaganda was in place to condemn any revolutionary said to be treasonous in following the French lead. To sympathize with the endeavours of America and France, or the wars of independence in Poland, Spain and Greece, was to be pro-revolutionary, and therefore anti-British.

Existentialism in Keats's poetry

Existentialism is a philosophy that centres upon the notion of the individual, and what it means to be in the world. Each human being is seen as isolated, having no connection with others, and living in an alien universe where there is no one purpose or inherent truth. In essence, it says that we each of us come from nothing, and live an absurd and meaningless life, ever moving towards the nothingness from which we came. At the beginning of the twentieth century, Jean-Paul Sartre popularized these ideas, arguing the importance of personal experience and responsibility, and the demands these make on the individual, who is ultimately a free agent in a seemingly meaningless universe. The philosophy rests upon the premise that personal experience is what influences an individual – time and history being necessary to existence – rather than reason. Living by such empirical, rather than theoretical, criteria leads us to interpret the present and gauge the future based on what has happened in the past.

Keats can be said to have anticipated existentialist philosophy in his work, with his emphasis on the pain and frustration caused by the inevitable realities of day-to-day existence, and the anguish of mortality. Indeed, in many of his poems, Keats does not wish to feel life too acutely. The transcendental qualities of indolence, sleep-inducing drugs or the power of the imagination seem more seductive options. However, he is a poet who always returns to reality, not least because – despite its temporary, ephemeral quality – there is a kind of permanence to be found in art. For that reason, Keats can seize the day.

Activity

Compare the ways in which Keats may be said to attempt to avoid reality in *Ode on Indolence* and *Ode to a Nightingale*.

Discussion

The reality of life brings suffering and despair. The two narrators, in their different ways, search for a method of escape. However, ultimately, the power of the imagination will lift the poet from his pain, with poetry offering the permanence he so craves.

Form, structure and language

Keats was the last of the Romantic poets to be born, and the first to die. In his brief lifetime, he wrote extensively and determinedly – almost as if he knew he had little time to produce the wealth of poetic work that he did. Beginning with lyrical fragments, he was soon producing the full lyrics, ballads and sonnets that would offer a foretaste of the odes that were to follow.

The lyric

The word 'lyric' comes from the Greek, signifying a song delivered to the accompaniment of a lyre. Today, the term refers to a poem that is brief and non-narrative in structure, presenting the reader with a compressed thought or emotion. Some lyrics present the narrator soliloquizing, expressing his thoughts in what appears to be a state of lonely isolation; others are more dramatic, and the narrator is seen to address someone in a set situation.

Lyrics can be organized in a multitude of different ways, depending on the subject matter and the narrator's supposed frame of mind. Keats uses the lyric to great effect, employing it in his sonnets, while more extended expressions of thought or mood are to be found in his elegies and meditative odes.

Activity

Describe some of the ways in which Keats makes use of the lyric in his own poetry.

Discussion

Keats can be seen to use the lyrical form in a variety of ways: the orderly, or even elaborately hyperbolic, love lyric; lyrical observances or meditations; and the deployed argument to justify a particular standpoint, value, or way of life.

Best known is the lyrical quality of his odes, which tends to convey his reflective and spiritual endeavours. *Ode to a Nightingale* focuses, for example, upon the immortality of the nightingale through its song, and the imaginative and ethereal quality of the verse lends it a lyrical aspect.

The music of the lyric comes across in a personal, first-person voice – and what we know of Keats's life and circumstances invites us to identify much of the lyrical outpouring with the poet himself. The lyrical sonnets, which offer us a brief snapshot of a mood or state of being, can also be seen to reflect the poet's life. *To my Brothers, To Haydon, On Sitting Down to Read King Lear Once Again* and *When I have Fears* are all rich in description and atmosphere, with the sense of acute observation and personal involvement often linked with the lyric.

The sonnet

The sonnet is a lyric poem, consisting of one stanza made up of 14 lines. Each line is in iambic pentameter (ten syllables with the basic rhythm consisting of an unstressed syllable followed by a stressed syllable). The rhyme scheme follows one of three distinct patterns:

- the Italian, or Petrarchan, sonnet, named after the fourteenth-century poet
- the English Shakespearean sonnet, first used by the Earl of Surrey
- the English Spenserian sonnet, named after the Renaissance poet Edmund Spenser.

Keats used all three variants. For example, in *On First Looking into Chapman's Homer*, Keats uses the Petrarchan sonnet form. The 14 lines are divided into two parts: an octave (the opening eight lines) with a rhyming pattern *abbaabba*, followed by a sestet (six lines) of a variant pattern (in this case, *cdcdcd*). In terms of content, the octave deals with the many texts of worth that the poet has read, while the sestet moves on to highlight the impact that George Chapman's translation of Homer has had upon him. The change in tone is marked by the colon and the ensuing word *Then*; such a 'turn', or change in direction, is known as the *volta*. This, and the sestet's extended simile, underscore the beauty that the poet finds in Chapman's pages. Note the change in the iambic pentameter beat in line 12; the extra syllable, and the altered stress pattern after the parenthetic pause, perhaps serve to emphasize the wonder at what has been discovered, both metaphorically in the sight of the Pacific Ocean and literally in Chapman's translation.

When I have Fears is an example of an English Shakespearean sonnet, whose form has been chosen for Keats's musings upon the solitariness of life. The structure is different, with three quatrains and a final couplet making up the rhyme scheme. The three quatrains are each a subordinate clause dependent upon the word *when*, while the concluding couplet is introduced by the word *then*. The opening *abab* quatrain has the narrator considering how fertile the imagination is, using harvest metaphors. The next four lines, *cdcd*, are about the amount of material at his disposal to be turned into poetry. The *efef* quatrain considers the temporary nature of love: and the fact that only three-and-a-half lines are devoted to this point, instead of four, perhaps shows that time is catching up with the poet. Only then does he turn his attention to the final refrain, in the *gg* couplet. Perhaps the fact that he devotes less sonnet space to love than to poetry shows us their comparative importance for him.

Activity

In *The Eve of St Agnes*, Keats uses a Spenserian stanzaic structure. What does this add to the poem?

Discussion

As a great admirer of Edmund Spenser, Keats opted to use the stanzaic shape of Spenser's *The Faerie Queene* – eight lines of iambic pentameter with a ninth extended to a 12-syllable iambic line (or alexandrine) – for his own narrative poem of 42 stanzas, *The Eve of St Agnes*. The length and slow movement of the structure lends itself well to such meditative epic verse, with the concluding alexandrine drawing out the meaning while denying quickness of pace. It is highly descriptive and sensuous, and every detail is enhanced by the interlinking rhyme scheme, *ababbcbcc*.

The rondeau

The rondeau is a poem of 10 or 13 lines with repeated lines running throughout, and only two rhyme sounds. A rondeau deals with a single subject, with a continued thematic repetition as in music. Keats wrote, in letters dated 16 December 1818 to 4 January 1819, that his poems *Fancy* and *Ode* are both 'specimens of a sort of rondeau', in whose form he could deal with a single idea 'with greater ease and more delight and freedom than in the sonnet'. There are obvious links between these poems and *Lines on the Mermaid Tavern*.

- Each poem deals with a single theme: *Fancy* with those impulses necessary for poetry, *Ode* with the *double-lived* immortality of poets, and *Lines on the Mermaid Tavern* with the notion of genius dwelling under one roof.
- Each has a four-stressed and predominantly trochaic pattern (one stressed syllable followed by one unstressed).
- Each is a short piece in which the opening lines are repeated as a refrain at the end.

However, not one of them is a true rondeau in terms of its strict definition.

Activity

How might it be argued that Keats's choice of a trochaic pattern in *Fancy* complements the meaning behind the poem?

Discussion

Keats may well have used trochees for the same reason that Shakespeare used them for his Weird Sisters in *Macbeth*. They can create the sense of an incantation or spell, so Keats is able to evoke the powerful or energetic force of the imagination (as Shakespeare's characters chant to raise evil spirits).

The rhyming couplets in the poem add to the mesmerizing rhythm, while the repetition of certain words and letters (especially the questions *What* and *Where*) stress the challenge of its rhythmic thrust. The irregularities in metre – in lines 11, 24, 34, 39, 48, 53, 71 and 89 – help to show the wanderings of fancy when allowed to roam free.

The ballad

Originally the ballad was a popular folk song that told a story; it was communicated orally and was very probably altered with every telling. Conventionally very dramatic, the ballad's focus was on the story and not the narrator – it was concentrated and concise, lacking any personal references. From this tradition was born the literary ballad. Famously, Wordsworth and Coleridge produced their *Lyrical Ballads* in 1798, emulating folk ballads in both form and style.

Keats's best-known work within this genre is *La Belle Dame sans Merci*, a ballad telling a medieval supernatural story taken from a fifteenth-century French poem by Alain Chartier. Keats is here emulating his favoured Renaissance poet, Edmund Spenser, who also wrote about the medieval world of myth and legend, and it has often been suggested that *The Faerie Queene*'s deceitful Duessa was the model for Keats's *Dame*. Luring men into her trap, Keats's evil enchantress seems to think nothing of the knight's love for her. This places the ballad firmly into the Petrarchan tradition.

Activity

The most common stanzaic form of a ballad alternates four and three stresses in iambic lines. Keats chooses to dispense with this, and instead makes each fourth line shorter, with only two stresses. Why does he do this, do you think?

Discussion

This shortened line (an iambic trimeter, rather than a tetrameter) makes each stanza seem more self-contained, fitting in with the simplicity of the overall language and lack of detail. For example:

> I see a lily on thy brow,
>> With anguish moist and fever-dew,
> And on thy cheeks a fading rose
>> Fast withereth too.   (9–12)

Here, the knight shows himself to be complicit in bringing on his own death, and the bluntness of the final line seems to further force this point home to the reader.

Activity

The use of repetition is a traditional feature of the ballad, and Keats makes much use of this in *La Belle Dame sans Merci*, to emphasize certain points. Discuss some examples.

Discussion

The most frequently repeated word is *pale* or *palely*, which occurs five times in the ballad. This makes the link between love and death definitive, cross-referencing to similar images of lilied brows, withering, wildness, starved lips and horrid warnings.

Interestingly, some of Keats's lines are repeated with slight modifications: for example, *The sedge has withered from the lake* (3) and *Though the sedge is withered from the lake* (47). It seems that here, Keats is marking the opening and closing of his ballad with the same words, in order to bring it full circle. He writes that, despite the landscape being unnatural, the knight's place is still to loiter there: the *Belle Dame* has weakened him past hope and care, and will haunt his mind forever.

The ode

Said to be Keats's most distinctive poetic achievement, the ode is, as M.H. Abrams describes it, 'serious in subject, elevated in style, and elaborate in its stanza structure' (*A Glossary of Literary Terms*). There are two classical models for odes: the Greek and the Roman. The Greek poet, Pindar, devised the former, original style, modelling it on dramatic choral songs. This meant that the stanzas followed a triadic or threefold pattern, with a *strophe* and *antistrophe* sharing the same metre, and an *epode* having another. Odes were produced to eulogize, praise or publicly celebrate a person, thing or belief.

The Horatian ode, produced by the Roman poet Horace, had a very different style and tone. Being shorter and homostrophic – in other words, having only one repeated stanza form – it was considered to be more serene and meditative for those who preferred a less bold and flamboyant style. The Romantic meditative ode was born of the two traditions, blending the irregularity and complexity of the Pindaric ode with the personal meditation of the Horatian ode.

All of Keats's odes were written in spring 1819 (March–June), with the exception of *To Autumn*, which was written a little later, in September of the same year. His brother Tom's death, along with his growing love for Fanny Brawne and deteriorating financial status and health, is often said to have contributed to the creation of these poems – which represent sensation and speculation, rather than thought. The order of writing is believed to be *Ode to Psyche*, *Ode to a Nightingale*, *Ode on a Grecian Urn*, *Ode on Melancholy*, *Ode on Indolence* and *To Autumn*, with each being Horatian in its uniform stanzaic structure, while complementing this with the more emotional, personal and intimate nature of the Pindaric ode.

Activity

In terms of structure, the complexity of the sonnet, with its designated rhyme scheme and its division into octave/sestet or quatrains/couplet, is found in some of the odes. Can you find examples?

Discussion

Since he experimented with the sonnet form for some time, it is not surprising that there are vestiges of this form in all of Keats's odes. The rhymes which link lines throughout, and the iambic pentameter beat, lend each ode the air of a sonnet, that 'little poem' from Italy.

The 67 lines of *Ode to Psyche*, the first of Keats's odes, are highly irregular, in terms of meter and rhyme scheme. The poem opens with a recognizable three-quatrain stanzaic pattern, of *abab cdcd efge* (note the absence of a couplet). These 12 lines have the sonnet's iambic pentameter, with the exception of the final line, which is brought up short on a three-foot pattern (trimeter). As the poem progresses, it becomes more and more irregular, with the rhyme scheme constantly changing and trimetrical lines making an appearance more and more frequently. The third stanza, despite having a very complex rhyme scheme, has the 14 lines of a sonnet: this is fitting, since this is the stanza that shows the poet in full adoration of his muse. The final 18-line stanza is a fitting close for a structurally variant poem which has the poet in a trance-like state throughout, as he considers Psyche to be his own soul powering his artistic imagination.

The ode that probably followed *Ode to Psyche* in composition was *Ode to a Nightingale*, and here Keats invented a new 10-line stanza. Opening with a quatrain based upon the Shakespearean sonnet (*abab*), he completed with a Petrarchan sestet (*cdecde*). A trimetrical eighth line completes the new form – and Keats must have been pleased with the effect, as he continued to use this structure in all the odes to follow.

Themes and ideas

Keats's beliefs are not easily summarized, but it is clear from what we have studied so far that he preoccupied himself with certain themes and ideas in his poetry. Some of these are more prevalent than others. What follows is not an exhaustive list, but discusses the dominant strains and ideologies that run throughout Keats's work.

Solitariness

Much writing of the Romantic period presents an isolated figure, alone with his thoughts and in a landscape that gives further inspiration to his art. In Wordsworth's *Lines written a few miles above Tintern Abbey* (1798), the narrator looks upon a *wild secluded scene* (6) as he links the setting with *Thoughts of more deep seclusion* (7). Mary Shelley's prose work, *Frankenstein* (1816), has at its centre three solitary narrators, whose solitariness leads to their demise. And Keats himself, in his early poems, wrote of isolated man, who experiences life alone and creates artistically in a solitary place:

> O solitude! if I must with thee dwell,
>   Let it not be among the jumbled heap
>   Of murky buildings; climb with me the steep –
> Nature's observatory – whence the dell,
> Its flowery slopes, its river's crystal swell,
>   May seem a span; let me thy vigils keep
>   'Mongst boughs pavilioned, where the deer's swift leap
> Startles the wild bee from the foxglove bell.
> But though I'd gladly trace these scenes with thee,
>   Yet the sweet converse of an innocent mind,
>   Whose words are images of thoughts refined,
> Is my soul's pleasure; and it sure must be
>   Almost the highest bliss of human-kind,
> When to thy haunts two kindred spirits flee.

The English literary critic and poet T.E. Hulme (1883–1917) considered the root of Romanticism to lie in the belief that it was only man's oppression that hindered progress in any walk of life. Infinite possibilities are available if, as Rousseau had argued, man can be free of constricting and tyrannical orders. Only then can the individual be free to dream of revolution. Essentially, he will begin to believe that he is a sort of god, able to create miracles on earth.

Activity

One of the Romantic values was individualism. Consider this idea with reference to Keats's *Ode to a Nightingale*.

Discussion

In *Ode to a Nightingale*, the narrator is a solitary figure, alone with the bird. From the outset – even before he is aware of the nightingale – the poet has numbed all feeling in order to disconnect himself from the pain of mortality. His *heart aches* (1), and this seems to be as a direct result of a world where:

> men sit and hear each other groan;
> Where palsy shakes a few, sad, last grey hairs,
> Where youth grows pale, and spectre-thin, and dies;
> Where but to think is to be full of sorrow   (24–27)

While listening to the nightingale, the poet becomes aware of a happiness that may be achieved from isolation. Despite insisting that he is not envious of the nightingale, it appears that he recognizes the bliss that comes of being ignorant of the realities of life. Wine is one method of numbing the pain, but *the blushful Hippocrene* is rejected in favour of escaping into a world of the imagination and fantasy. The nightingale's song becomes a symbol of the poet's relief, and a muse to inspire him. As the song fades, he is left wondering whether he really heard the nightingale's song at all; nonetheless, the very thought of it symbolizes the artist's work – a solitary endeavour, which it must be if it is to be in any way visionary.

Death and immortality

While Keats's earlier poems dealt with the appreciation of material beauty, his later work was very much bound up with ideas of death and decay. Matthew Arnold wrote that Keats was consumed by the principle of beauty as truth, but that 'he had terrible bafflers – consuming disease and early death'. Alluding to one of Keats's letters, Arnold argues that Keats's poetry was hindered by a lack of experience in the short term: '[I am] young, and writing at random, straining after particles of light in the midst of a great darkness'. He was becoming so concerned with illness and, after the death of his brother Tom, he was so grief-stricken, he could no longer write to his surviving brother in America. Essentially, Keats was trying to isolate himself from his own morbid obsession with death. In a letter to Fanny Brawne, he spoke of feeling destined to die young, and this concern was reinforced by the history of tuberculosis in his family: 'I have never known any unalloy'd Happiness for many days together: the death or sickness of some one has always spoilt my hours'

(July 1819). Duncan Wu considers Keats's conviction that his life would be short to be his motivation: 'Fearing that he did not have long to live, he laboured furiously, developed with abnormal rapidity and, in what time he had, produced some of the finest poetry of the period' (*Romanticism: An Anthology*).

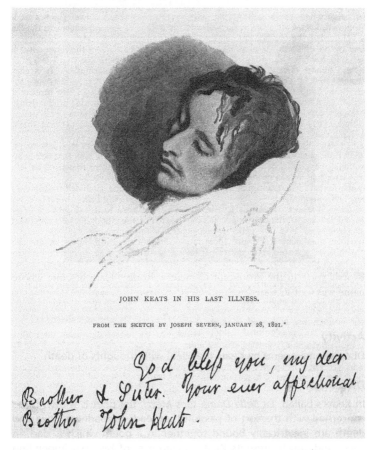

JOHN KEATS IN HIS LAST ILLNESS.

FROM THE SKETCH BY JOSEPH SEVERN, JANUARY 28, 1821.*

Keats on his deathbed, by Joseph Severn, who noted: 'Drawn to keep me awake – a deadly sweat was on him all this night'

Keats's grave in the Protestant Cemetery, Rome: 'Here lies one whose name was writ in water'

Activity

Discuss some poems by Keats that deal with thoughts of death.

Discussion

In Keats's ballad, *La Belle Dame sans Merci*, the poet is shown to be concerned with the sort of passion that leads to madness. Love and death are inextricably bound together in a poem which is dark in tone, and which presents Keats's awareness of his own impending death. The conclusion has the knight forever trapped in a nightmare of unfulfilled love.

In much the same vein, *Lamia* is about a heroine who is beautiful, yet false, in a version of the myth which has Keats add Lycius's death in order to reinforce the tragedy. The unfinished epic *Hyperion* presents loss and suffering through the exile of the Titans by their own offspring. Although incomplete, it shows the destined painful dethronement of Hyperion by Apollo.

Such loss is the theme of *The Eve of St Agnes*, which sees misery born of the ecstasy of love; while *Ode on Melancholy* paints the image of a mistress with *peerless* beauty, behind whose façade there lies only death. Finally, in perhaps Keats's most famous poem, *Ode to a Nightingale*, he writes of being *half in love with easeful Death* (52), seeing it as a blissful alternative to the agonies of life.

Nature

Keats's poetry all alludes to the natural world, from his early lyrical fragments to the odes of 1819; indeed, even his letters often incorporate natural images and descriptions:

> I go among the Feilds and catch a glimpse of a stoat or a fieldmouse peeping out of the withered grass – the creature hath a purpose and its eyes are bright with it – I go amongst the buildings of a city and I see a Man hurrying along – to what? the Creature has a purpose and his eyes are bright with it.
>
> (19 March 1819)

Many of Keats's poems show an awareness of his natural surroundings and the forces of nature at work. His early studies in medicine meant that he also had scientific knowledge that could be applied to his countless references to animals and plants.

Activity

In *To Autumn*, Keats's powers of observation are acute. How does he reveal his attention to the detail of his natural surroundings?

Discussion

As ever, Keats evokes the senses in order to convey his thoughts more specifically. By concentrating not only on sight, but also on sound, smell and touch, he is better able to use nature as a link with the human world, for example in lines 27–33.

Edmund Spenser greatly influenced Keats's work, and he used many Spenserian poetic techniques. Spenser's nature imagery was idealized and simple, and Keats emulates this style – often using it for allegorical effect, as did Spenser. He uses the interlinking rhyme scheme that Spenser made his own, thus linking ideas throughout the stanza.

The power of the imagination

For Keats, the imagination was everything, as it provides the poet with the ability to access the truth – a state that he considered to be a heightened reality, that went beyond what is experienced in everyday life. In a letter to Richard Woodhouse, Keats wrote: 'A Poet is the most unpoetical of any thing in existence; because he has no Identity – he is continually in for – and filling some other Body' (27 October 1818). For Keats, it was imperative that the poet submerge his sense of self in 'negative capabilities', a phrase coined by Keats himself which meant the point at which a person is capable of being in uncertainties, mysteries and doubts, without always striving for facts and reasons. Only then can the poet hope to imaginatively engage with his subject, and discover 'essential beauty' or 'truth'.

Love and sexuality

In his poetry, love was a major theme for Keats – although the focus is always upon the transience of its intensity. We have already considered how Keats thought that love may interfere with his poetical prowess, and that his deep feelings for Fanny Brawne distressed him because of this. However, just as his love for her never died, his ability to write about love continued to develop. As Keats's poetic style grew, he tried to become the 'negatively capable' writer, one who writes objectively leaving no traces of his own life or ego. What interested Keats was that his readers should obtain some sort of feeling from his work. Of *Lamia*, for example, a mythological love story, he wrote, 'I am certain there is that sort of fire in it which must take hold of people in some way – give them either pleasant or unpleasant sensation. What they want is a sensation of some sort' (September 1819).

Activity

To what extent is *Ode on Melancholy* a significant love poem?

Discussion

Many critics see Fanny Brawne in this ode, being the *mistress* who demonstrates her anger and raves when the fit takes her. Jean H. Hagstrum argues that this is particularly relevant, as here, 'Keats gives utterance to that central quality of sexual love we have observed as present in his sensibility from the very first: that it is deeply paradoxical and therefore inevitably oxymoronic in its literary expression' (*The Romantic Body: Love and Sexuality in Keats, Wordsworth, and Blake*). In the third stanza, Keats forces us to face reality once more, when he tells us that his mistress:

> dwells with Beauty – Beauty that must die;
> And Joy, whose hand is ever at his lips
> Bidding adieu; and aching Pleasure nigh,
> Turning to poison while the bee-mouth sips:
> Ay, in the very temple of Delight
> Veiled Melancholy has her sovran shrine   (21–26)

Melancholy is found to descend suddenly, in an ever-changing world – and, here, Keats links it to love, beauty and the transience of pleasures.

Critical views

The first generation of Romantic poets, with the exception of Blake, all achieved success in their own lifetimes. Of the second generation, only Byron gained a good literary reputation, while Keats and Shelley achieved recognition only after death.

Immediately following Keats's death, a succession of events and damning obituaries further tarnished his name, and put him out of the literary gaze for some time. Without meaning to, Fanny Brawne damaged his reputation. Hearing that a biography might be written about him, she expressed her wish that his memory remain only with her and those who were close to him. Desperate to save his reputation from further blackening, she ironically sent out the message that Keats's work should be condemned to obscurity.

Blackwood's continued to attack him posthumously, scoffing at his politics, his poetry and even his gravestone epitaph. Keats's critics were stalwarts, even after his death, condemning him for being a cockney, for his humble beginnings, for his failure to be university educated, and because he championed radical notions. What annoyed *Blackwood's*, and the Tory press as a whole, was 'Keats's bold vocabulary of political, aesthetic, and cultural reform, in the arena of the reformist press – this upstart graduate of Hunt's new school issuing a liberal challenge to the prevailing social, political, and moral order' (John Kandle, 'The Politics of Keats's Early Poetry', in *The Cambridge Companion to Keats*, edited by Susan J. Wolfson).

Shelley's *Adonis* (1821) attempted to right some critical wrongs, by suggesting that Keats's death was hastened by poor reviews at the latter stages of his life. Critics seized upon this notion, and further fuelled the idea that Keats had been an effeminate individual, whose weaknesses as a man were translated into his poetry.

In the spring of 1821, John Taylor was adamant in his defence of his friend, and determined to put together a biography. However, squabbles among the very people who knew and loved him only served to create a deadlock situation, so Keats's reputation continued to lack favour and his name drifted further out of the poetic arena. In 1829 the tide began to turn, however, on the back of strong praise from respected figures such as William Hazlitt:

> **[Keats] gave the greatest promise of genius of any poet of his day. He displayed extreme tenderness, beauty, originality and delicacy of fancy; all he wanted was manly strength and fortitude to reject the temptations of singularity in sentiment and expression. Some of his shorter and later pieces are, however, as free from faults as they are full of beauties.**
>
> *(Select British Poets*, 1824)

The growing fame of the poet Alfred Tennyson meant that his words of praise for Keats were taken seriously. Following this, Richard Monckton Milnes produced the long-overdue Keats biography in 1848, drawing in still further good reviews about Keats, the man and the poet.

From the second half of the nineteenth century onwards, various literary figures – such as Robert Browning, Matthew Arnold, Charles Dickens, the Rossettis, Elizabeth Barrett Browning, Gerard Manley Hopkins and W.B. Yeats – championed what had once been viewed as a lost cause. Although he was initially praised as a gentle, sentimental and rather lightweight poet, Keats's reputation steadily grew until, with the admiration of Wilfred Owen during the First World War, Keats's poetic genius was no longer called into question.

Praised by critical heavyweights such as T.S. Eliot and Samuel Beckett, Keats's reputation gained the stature it deserved in the twentieth century – he even acquired a legion of female fans, the audience he had always insisted on rejecting.

Today, Keats is considered a major Romantic poet, standing alongside such poets as Wordsworth and Blake in importance and strength. Literary critics have considered his poetry in many fascinating contexts, and illuminating biographies of the man and his work, such as Andrew Motion's *Keats* (1997), have emerged to humanize and further enhance the experience of Keats's poetry for modern readers.

Essay Questions

Worked questions

The two questions below are followed by some points you might address in your response.

1   'Pain is an integral part of Keats's vision' (J.C. Smith). Discuss this statement in relation to at least *one* long poem, or *three* of Keats's shorter poems.

As long as your chosen poems are relevant to the question, it is up to you to choose which to focus on. Once you have made that decision, you need to consider the main points of your answer. A plan is always advisable. Here are a few ideas to get you started.

The most obvious poems to start with are the odes, as all are concerned with the poet himself and the power of the imagination. *Ode on Melancholy*, for example, makes the claim that joy and sorrow have a close relationship and that, in order to appreciate the aesthetically beautiful, one must first contemplate the painful notion that it will one day die or disappear. *Ode to a Nightingale* follows much the same line of thought, with its musings upon the impermanence of life. In this ode, Keats suggests that, if the nightingale is to be seen as a symbol of the poetic imagination, life does indeed have a sort of permanence through art. This may lead you to consider the ambiguous aphorism that concludes *Ode on a Grecian Urn*, and whether or not art ('beauty') does produce the only permanence ('truth') to be found on earth.

Of course, many other poems have the theme of pain. *La Belle Dame sans Merci*, *Lamia* and *The Eve of St Agnes* each present romantic love as closely aligned with loss and suffering; the longer poems, such as *Endymion* and *Hyperion*, portray pain on an epic scale through mythology. Duncan Wu says of the latter, '*The Fall of Hyperion* suggests that he was coming to agree with Wordsworth that "Suffering is permanent, obscure, and dark,/And has the nature of infinity"' ('Keats and the "Cockney School"', in *The Cambridge Companion to Keats*, edited by Susan J. Wolfson).

It is always important to root poetry in its social context, and Keats's obsession with mortality was, perhaps, born out of his own family bereavements: the untimely deaths of his parents and brother. His own state of continuing ill-health only added to this preoccupation. Similarly, his situation as a struggling poet caused him financial and emotional hardship, as he sought to maintain a living and secure a marriage to Fanny Brawne. Indeed, there are critics who feel sure that Keats was frustrated by his unconsummated affair with his fiancée.

Keats's philosophy was that beauty and pleasure could only ever truly be experienced in relation to suffering: to pursue the aesthetics of beauty is an illusion, and ignores the reality of the pain of life. Keats did not believe in the Christian ideology of the 'vale of tears', whereby the suffering in this life would be redeemed in an afterlife. Rather, he thought it was possible to lift the soul to another level on earth, experiencing joy only after experiencing pain. Perhaps pain could only be healed through the use of the imagination – but even then, there are poems where Keats shows his uncertainty as to whether even his poetic art has the energy to heal suffering permanently.

2 **It has been said that Keats's verse looks at an idealized world picture that is firmly rooted in the considerations of Romanticism. Do you agree?**

With a question like this, it is necessary for you to provide a definition of 'Romanticism' as a frame of reference for your choice of poems. The main points to remember about Romanticism are:

- there is not one overriding definition of the term, and the so-called 'school' of Romantic poets spans decades, encompassing different beliefs and styles
- the term was coined well after the Romantics themselves were dead

- it is a literary 'school' firmly rooted in a historical context
- of the traits that the Romantics do have in common, the most important are the goals of individualism, freedom, imagination, sincerity, spontaneity and imaginative truths.

In your choice of poems you should go on to evidence the above features. Whichever poems you choose, remember that Keats was first and foremost a visual poet, subjecting himself – and his readers – to the impact of the senses. His focus was always on the power of the imagination to provide freedom from the suffering of life. Keats saw futility behind most of what life has to offer, and finding a voice through poetry may well have been his answer to immortalizing a sense of self.

Sample questions

The following questions are for you to try.

1 Examine the ways in which Keats shows his love of the natural world.
2 Discuss some of the themes that Keats might be trying to convey in his narrative poems.
3 Discuss some ways in which Keats's philosophy 'Beauty is truth' is applied in his poetry.
4 Explore Keats's ability to adapt classical myth and legend in his poems. You should refer to **one** of the longer poems, or a **selection** of shorter ones.
5 Keats wrote, 'I have been reading over a part of a short poem I have composed lately call'd *Lamia* – and I am certain there is that sort of fire in it which must take hold of people in some way – give them either pleasant or unpleasant sensation. What they want is a sensation of some sort.' Do you agree with Keats's view about readers' expectations of poetry, and his assessment of *Lamia*?

6 In what ways can Keats's odes be considered philosophical?
7 By detailed reference to at least **two** poems, indicate in what ways Keats might be seen as a love poet.
8 To what extent can Keats's work display a belief in the power of the imagination, and a rejection of reason and ordered rationality?
9 What features of subject matter and style show Keats to have a desperate yearning to escape from the harsh reality of life?
10 In his letters, Keats wrote: 'Death is the great divorcer for ever'. Consider Keats's obsession with death in his poetry, both in terms of subject matter and style.

Chronology

Events in Keats's life

1795 Born 31 October, son of Thomas Keats, manager of a livery stable.

1803 Enters John Clarke's school, Enfield.

1804 Father dies. Mother remarries. Keats and his siblings go to live with mother's parents in Edmonton.

1810 Mother dies of tuberculosis. Meets Cowden Clarke.

1811 Apprenticed to Thomas Hammond, an apothecary-surgeon.

Historical events

1783 American War of Independence ends.

1789 French Revolution starts.

1792 French king executed. Britain goes to war with France: Napoleonic wars.

1794 Blake: *Songs of Innocence and Experience* published in one volume.

1795 Protests against the war. Protests for Parliamentary reform. Crop failures, bread shortages and inflation.

1798 Wordsworth and Coleridge: *Lyrical Ballads*.

1803 War with France resumes.

1804 Napoleon becomes Emperor. First Corn Laws.

1808 Leigh Hunt founds *The Examiner*.

1809 Birth of Charles Darwin. *Quarterly Review* founded.

1810 The slave trade abolished in Britain.

1811 George, the Prince of Wales, acts as regent for George III, who has been declared insane.

1812 Luddite riots.

Events in Keats's life

1816 Qualifies to practise medicine. Meets John Hamilton Reynolds, Leigh Hunt and Benjamin Haydon.
First published poem, O Solitude, appears in The Examiner.

1817 Gives up medicine for poetry.
First volume published.

1818 Endymion and Hyperion.
Walking tour of northern England and Scotland.
Brother, Tom, dies of tuberculosis.
Moves into Wentworth Place.
Meets Fanny Brawne.

1819 Writes some of his most famous odes, The Eve of St Agnes and Lamia.
Secretly engaged to Fanny Brawne.
Early signs of tuberculosis.

1820 Severe haemorrhage. Travels to Rome.

1821 Dies 23 February.

Historical events

1815 Battle of Waterloo. End of Napoleonic Wars. Corn Laws.

1816 Game Laws.

1819 Byron: Don Juan Cantos I & II.
Massacre at St Peter's Fields.

1820 George IV crowned.

1821 Shelley: Adonais in Pisa. More liberal policies from Lord Liverpool.

1822 Shelley drowns off Livorno; his body is identified by the copy of Keats's latest poems in his pocket.

Further Reading

M. H. Abrams, *A Glossary of Literary Terms* (Holt, Rinehart and Winston, 1988)

John Barnard, *John Keats* (Cambridge University Press, 1987)

Harold Bloom (ed.), *Modern Critical Views: John Keats* (Chelsea House Publishers, 1985)

Marilyn Butler, *Romantics, Rebels, and Reactionaries: English Literature and its Background 1760–1830* (Oxford University Press, 1982)

Stephen Copley and John Whale (eds.), *Beyond Romanticism: New Approaches to Texts and Contexts 1780–1832* (Routledge, 1992)

Jeffrey N. Cox, *Poetry and Politics in the Cockney School: Keats, Shelley, Hunt and Their Circle* (Cambridge University Press, 1998)

Richard Cronin, *The Politics of Romantic Poetry: In Search of the Pure Commonwealth* (Macmillan, 2000)

Stuart Curran (ed.), *The Cambridge Companion to British Romanticism* (Cambridge University Press, 1993)

Aiden Day, *Romanticism* (Routledge, 1996)

Robert Gittings, *Letters of John Keats* (Oxford University Press, 1987)

Jean H. Hagstrum, *The Romantic Body: Love and Sexuality in Keats, Wordsworth, and Blake* (University of Tennessee Press, 1985)

T.E. Hulme, 'Romanticism and Classicism', in Herbert Read (ed.), *Speculations, Essays on Humanism and the Philosophy of Art*, 2nd edn. (Routledge and Kegan Paul, 1936)

Marjorie Levinson, *Keats's Life of Allegory: The Origins of a Style* (Oxford University Press, 1989)

Thomas McFarland, *The Masks of Keats: The Endeavour of a Poet* (Oxford University Press, 2000)

Andrew Motion, *Keats* (Faber and Faber, 1997)

Paul O'Flinn, *How to Study Romantic Literature* (Macmillan, 1988)

Michael O'Neill (ed.), *Keats: Bicentenary Readings* (Edinburgh University Press, 1997)

Stephen Prickett (ed.), *The Romantics* (Methuen, 1981)

Nicholas Roe, *John Keats and the Culture of Dissent* (Clarendon Press, 1997)

Nicholas Roe (ed.), *Keats and History* (Cambridge University Press, 1995)

H. E. Rollins (ed.), *The Letters of John Keats* (Harvard University Press, 1958)

H. E. Rollins (ed.), *The Keats Circle: Letters and Papers* and *More Letters and Poems of the Keats Circle*, 2 volumes (Harvard University Press, 1965)

Brian Stone, *The Poetry of Keats* (Penguin, 1992)

Helen Vendler, *The Odes of John Keats* (Harvard University Press, 1983)

Daniel P. Watkins, *Keats's Poetry and the Politics of the Imagination* (Associated University Presses, 1989)

Susan J. Wolfson (ed.), *The Cambridge Companion to Keats* (Cambridge University Press, 2001)

Duncan Wu (ed.), *Romanticism: An Anthology*, 3rd edn. (Blackwell, 2006)

Index of Titles and First Lines

Titles

First lines